CHIVA-SOM'S
THAI SPA CUISINE

MANAGING EDITOR/PHOTOGRAPHY DIRECTOR
MELISA TEO

EDITOR
JOANNA GREENFIELD

DESIGNERS
LISA DAMAYANTI/YOLANDE LIM

PRODUCTION MANAGER
SIN KAM CHEONG

First published in 2005 by **EDITIONS DIDIER MILLET PTE LTD**
for **CHIVA-SOM INTERNATIONAL HEALTH RESORTS CO., LTD**
73/4 Petchkasem Road, Hua Hin
Prachuab Khirikhan 77110, Thailand
Head Office: 11th floor, Modern Town Building
87 Sukhumvit 63, Bangkok 10110, Thailand
Email: bkkoff@chivasom.com
Website: www.chivasom.com

This edition published in 2011

EDITIONS DIDIER MILLET PTE LTD
121 Telok Ayer Street, #03-01
Singapore 068590
www.edmbooks.com

Photographs © 2005 Jörg Sundermann
© 2005 Editions Didier Millet Pte Ltd

Printed in Singapore.

ISBN 978-981-4155-73-1

CHIVA-SOM'S
THAI SPA CUISINE

Recipes by Chef Paisarn Cheewinsiriwat and his culinary team
Photography by Jörg Sundermann
Introduction by Aun Koh

CONTENTS

INTRODUCTION

SPA CUISINE

For centuries, people have gone to spas. and since those early years, spa styles and cultures have continually developed and evolved. Spa cuisine, however, seemed to get left behind. Many spas offered healthy food, food that was great for the body but it was food that left guests unsatisfied or upset. Indeed, spa food in the latter half of the 20th century was commonly thought of as only one step better than hospital food. Even worse, well-intentioned but misguided restaurateurs and chefs in the 1980s went so far as to promote what they dubbed a Californian spa cuisine.

SPA FOOD IN THE LATTER HALF OF THE 20TH CENTURY WAS COMMONLY THOUGHT OF AS ONLY ONE STEP BETTER THAN HOSPITAL FOOD.

But as time moved on, attitudes towards spa cuisine changed and Chiva-Som was quick to pick up on it. Firstly, when choosing a live-in retreat, Chiva-Som saw that customers made choices not just on how good a property's facilities or treatments were, but on how good their meals were going to be. Also, Chiva-Som knew that their well-heeled patrons were not only interested in food that was good for them, but food that actually tasted great too. Most of their customers wined and dined at some of the world's best restaurants. They had well-developed palates and if they were to eat something really healthy, they would like it to be on a par with the gourmet meals they were used to.

CHIVA-SOM'S INNOVATIONS

Chiva-Som's innovative Thai spa cuisine evolved with this kind of traveller in mind. And the great importance placed on spa cuisine at Chiva-Som has delivered delicious and healthy food which the resort is now famous for. This newly structured and defined spa cuisine is guided by a few simple principles. Firstly, to reduce fats and avoid cooking with oil if possible. Secondly to reduce the intake of salt. And lastly, to add as much raw food and complex carbohydrates into the diet as possible. To achieve these objectives, the chefs have developed a few simple techniques that people can easily adopt at home. Instead of cooking with oil, for example, food should be cooked with Chiva-Som's reduced vegetable stock. This stock—which recipe you will find in the Basics section—is healthy, light and easy to make. It is also one of the foundations of this cuisine, and in order to cook a great number of the dishes in this book, you will have to learn how to make it. A few dishes that illustrate the principle of lowering fat content are Chiva-Som's takes on the following classic Thai dishes.

Firstly, the Thai green curry involves cooking the curry paste in reduced vegetable stock instead of stir-frying it in heated oil, as it is traditionally done. Also, reducing the fat intake even more, the use of coconut milk is minimized meaning less fat whilst retaining lots of flavour. The health benefits of coconut milk have just been claimed by scientists but there is an even healthier alternative: a combination of low fat milk and young coconut water can be used instead of full coconut milk. Finally, the proportion of curry to meat is also different. In most restaurants, an order of green curry with chicken is a bowl of the curry sauce, with a few pieces of chicken—it's more gravy than meat. At Chiva-Som, an order of chicken curry will result in a plate of beautifully cooked chicken breast, with curry lightly sauced over. The curry sauce is not the main ingredient but is used to flavour the chicken. With this simple dish, the first—and perhaps most important—of Chiva-Som's spa cuisine's principles are easily illustrated. Fats are reduced substantially

and the use of vegetable stock completely replaces any need for oil. Another dish which has been healthily re-created to reduce the fat content is Chiva-Som's delicious satay sauce. Instead of peanuts, the chefs use almonds, whose essential fatty acids are healthier than those of normal nuts. They are also used as a precaution against possible allergic reactions. In addition to this substitution, the sauce is flavoured with tamarind juice, used not only to add flavour, but as a healthy shortening agent.

Yet another great recipe, healthily re-created, is Thai poached chicken salad.

WELL-HEELED PATRONS WERE NOT ONLY INTERESTED IN FOOD THAT WAS GOOD FOR THEM, BUT FOOD THAT ACTUALLY TASTED GREAT TOO.

Traditionally, the chicken should be poached in coconut milk, but at Chiva-Som, the chicken is poached in soy milk, a much healthier option. Where possible, coconut milk is reduced. For example, in three of the resort's signature salads, winged bean and scallop salad, banana blossom salad, and prawn and pomelo salad, the traditional coconut milk dressing is substituted for one

 SALT

Salt leads to high blood pressure. By steaming food, the natural flavours emerge and salt is not needed. If salt is necessary use soy sauce instead.

 FAT

Following Chiva-Som's simple guidelines means it is easy to reduce fat intake. Firstly, food is cooked in reduced vegetable stock rather than oil. Coconut milk should always be minimized. Interesting dressings need not be fat-based; instead, combine fresh ingredients such as lime juice and honey with soy sauce. Steaming foods is a much healthier and tastier way to cook.

 RAW

Raw foods are an important part of anyone's diet as most are complex carbohydrates. As a great source of fibre, raw foods also have a greater variety of flavours, making them very versatile. Apple juice is commonly used in place of sugar at Chiva-Som. And vegetables are either raw or only slightly cooked in order to keep the goodness of the ingredient.

made from soy sauce, lime juice and honey, proof that dressing can be tasty without adding any extra fat.

Another staple of Thai cuisine, like green curry, is paad Thai. However, paad Thai is oily and rich. Here, just as the aromatics for the curry were cooked with vegetable stock, the paad Thai is similarly stir-fried in the vegetable stock. Furthermore, only egg whites are used, so as to reduce cholesterol intake.

This technique, frying with reduced vegetable stock, is perhaps one of the most important techniques you will learn from this book, and it's something the resort's chefs return to over and over again. Of course, food need not always be fried. In fact, the Chiva-Som chefs advocate steaming foods. Not only is it a healthier method of cooking, but it also allows for the natural flavours in the food to emerge. This is good because much of Chiva-Som's cuisine is also predicated on the lowering of salt.

Too much salt in one's diet, as any nutritionist will tell you, may lead to water retention and can contribute to high blood pressure. Learning to cook with less salt can, over time, make you much healthier. And if you use foods that are loaded with natural flavours, you will find that you won't miss the salt. In fact, as salt and fat intake are lowered, what many Chiva-Som guests have discovered is a renewed palate. They discover that they are able to taste more and more subtle flavours. Which, again, comes as no surprise to the resort's nutritionists.

SALT AND FAT MASK FLAVOURS AND A DIET TOO RICH IN EITHER IS ONE IN WHICH MUCH NUANCE IS OFTEN LOST.

RAW FOODS HAVE A GREATER RANGE OF FLAVOURS, IN PARTICULAR SWEET FLAVOURS, THAT CAN BE INCORPORATED INTO THAI FOOD AND USED TO REPLACE SUGAR.

Both salt and fat mask flavours and a diet too rich in either is one in which much nuance is often lost. If, however salt is necessary, use low sodium soy sauce instead.

The last principle that the chefs at Chiva-Som adopt is to include as much raw healthier wild rice or brown rice. Even when making desserts; Chiva-Som's mango and sticky rice uses black rice, for example.

The recipes in this book are built upon these simple ideas and techniques. Some will require a little bit of practice, others just a bit of understanding. Essentially, the food presented here is delicious Thai food, made healthy. And as you look through these pages, you'll be able to learn not just some skills to making Thai

THE AVERAGE PERSON NEEDS APPROXIMATELY 2,000 CALORIES A DAY.

food and other complex carbohydatrates in your diet as possible. Chiva-Som's Thai spa cuisine uses a lot of raw foods. This is because not only are they good for the body, but raw foods have a greater range of flavours, in particular sweet flavours, that can be incorporated into Thai food and used to replace sugar. These can range from raw vegetables and fruit themselves to juices. In fact, one of the best sugar substitutes is apple juice. As a sweetener for soups, stir-fries and curries, it is fantastic. Honey is also a great natural sweetener that is used extensively at Chiva-Som and in the recipes in this book.

Complex carbohydrates should be used in place of processed and refined carbohydrates. These are far better for digestion as they are higher in fibre. It's also a relatively easy substitution, such as switching from white rice to the much

spa cuisine, but the rationale behind it. And these general principles deserve to be stated up front.

LIFESTYLE CHANGES

While this book is a great guide and will without a doubt, if used well, enhance your health, no book is a substitute for a personal consultation with a trained nutritionist. Everyone's body is slightly different and what each person needs to eat to become fitter is thus unique. For some, the biggest change might be in their routine—when and what meals are eaten. For others, it might be the kinds of foods they are eating—too many carbohydrates in the evening or not enough raw fruit and vegetables, for example. That said, there are a few general principles that should help anyone.

First, most people eat too much. Portion size is something taken very seriously by the nutritionists at Chiva-Som. And while they know that counting calories can be a real pain, they ask their guests to consider two things. The average person needs approximately 2,000 calories a day (as a very rough guide to finding your own requirement multiply your weight in kilos by 30) and any portion of meat, poultry or fish no larger than the length and width of a person's palm (which is around 100g/3½ oz) is probably about right. Studies have shown that the average person's calorie intake is far too high, much higher than the recommended daily amount. So while it's not necessary to count the calories of every little thing one eats, it helps to keep in mind the total daily allowance when deciding what and how much to eat at each meal. Which is actually pretty easy to do. It's simply a matter of recognizing, for example, that a lunch rounded off with a small dessert or accompanied by a glass of wine means that dinner that evening has to be much lower in calories and more nutritious.

Speaking of excess, Chiva-Som's nutritionists also warn that most people eat too much fat. For many, 50 per cent of their calorie intake comes from fat, and often from saturated (the 'bad') fat and hydrogenated oils (the 'bad' oils). They recommend lowering the percentage of calories from fat to 30 per cent and focusing on a higher intake of healthy essential fatty acids.

THE KNOW-HOW

The biggest challenge, by far, faced by Chiva-Som's nutritionists has not been in helping to plan the resort's menus. It is equipping guests with the knowledge on how to continue to eat properly after leaving the spa. This is done, firstly through consultations, secondly through the food itself and lastly with cooking classes. This

AS A VERY ROUGH GUIDE TO FINDING YOUR OWN CALORIE REQUIREMENT, MULTIPLY YOUR WEIGHT IN KILOS BY 30.

approach provides guests with the essential knowledge on why, what and how to eat healthily with Chiva-Som's spa cuisine. That is another reason why it is so very important that the food has to taste as good as it does. It is quite difficult to change a lifestyle if the food is not so appealing. It is a rather daunting task. But if the food is delicious, so delicious in fact that one forgets that it is 'healthy', then making long-term lifestyle changes can be quite simple. Half the battle has already been won. The other half is

IT'S NOT NECESSARY
TO COUNT THE
CALORIES OF EVERY
LITTLE THING ONE
EATS. KEEP IN MIND
THE TOTAL DAILY
ALLOWANCE WHEN
DECIDING WHAT AND
HOW MUCH TO EAT
AT EACH MEAL.

truss a chicken, de-bone a pig's trotter, determine the best grade of flour for specific kinds of pasta, or identify ingredients you've never heard of before. There are cookbooks that tell stories, with wonderful essays interspersed throughout. Reading these vignettes creates a bond with the chef or author and cooking the dishes feels like a visit from an old friend. Then there are the trusted books that you turn to on a regular basis. The books whose recipes you use the most, whose tips you rely on the most, whose explanations you like best, and whose cooking principles you have adopted as your own.

CHIVA-SOM'S APPROACH

This book is meant to fall into this last and most rare of categories. It's a book you can use every day. The recipes in here are delicious and surprisingly easy to use. You'll be surprised at how quickly you can master Thai spa cuisine, and how amazed your friends and family will be when you start serving them these wonderful dishes. This book is also a reference tool, with information on Thai spices, herbs and ingredients. There's nutritional information that can help you plan or re-plan your regular diet. And there are techniques that you can adopt and use, no matter what kind of cuisine you are cooking.

becoming equipped with some knowledge about food, making the commitment, and gaining the confidence needed to ask for a half-portion or a salad instead of fries or dressing on the side.

The purpose of this book is to enable and motivate those who need or want to make changes in their life. Cookbooks fall into a variety of categories. Some are splashy, with lush, gorgeous photographs but impossible recipes. These are vanity books, written by famed chefs and restaurateurs in attempts to show off their culinary prowess. There are reference books, huge tomes of data that you can turn to when trying to figure out how to

And that, more than anything, is why this book has been written. It's meant to be your companion and guide; it's meant to inspire you. But at the same time, it's not meant to be too prescriptive. It's not meant to tell you what you can and cannot have. Nor is it trying to sell you any kind of labelled programme. This is not a fad diet that you'll lose patience with. It's simply, as the chefs and nutritionists at Chiva-Som see it, a smart and healthy way to eat.

At the resort itself, these same chefs and nutritionists try to refrain from writing prescriptive diets for their guests, even after seeing them in personal consultations. Instead, they act as guides, offering helpful tips and making suggestions that they know will not be too strange, too radical or too difficult for these guests to adopt.

The diet the nutritionists try and encourage their guests to take up is not a quick fix either. Instead of trying to help them shed a lot of weight overnight, they help them eat healthier foods and become more aware of themselves. It may take some people longer to lose weight, or to feel more energetic, but in the long run, these people will have a smaller chance of yo-yoing back to their heavier selves; they'll also feel better for longer. These changes in eating habits that follow the principles behind Chiva-Som's Thai spa cuisine are changes that a person must agree (with him or herself) to make for the long haul. It's not just a matter of eating only steak for a month. It's a matter of changing one's life.

This book represents only one aspect—an extremely important one though—of the total Chiva-Som experience. You can use it for what it is on the surface, a fantastic new and healthy way of cooking Thai food, or you can delve deeper. You can begin to explore the science behind the way the food is prepared. You can also begin to think about the philosophies behind the healthy lifestyle this book is promoting. You will find that this book and the Chiva-Som philosophy behind Thai spa cuisine will open up new possibilities for you, and will help you make permanent changes you didn't think were possible.

IT MAY TAKE SOME PEOPLE LONGER TO LOSE WEIGHT, OR TO FEEL MORE ENERGETIC, BUT IN THE LONG RUN, THESE PEOPLE HAVE A SMALLER CHANCE OF YO-YOING BACK TO THEIR HEAVIER SELVES.

SNACKS

Food is important in Thai culture and Thai people love to snack, no matter what time of day. Eating small meals frequently throughout the day is also recommended by Chiva-Som's nutritionists. The right type of snack eaten mid-morning and mid-afternoon raises the metabolism, which aids weight loss and keeps blood sugar levels balanced. These light and tasty snacks can be eaten on their own or as an accompaniment to main dishes.

BETEL LEAF WRAPS
MIANG KHAM

Makes 20 pieces

NUTRIENTS PER PIECE

Energy 23.3 kcal

Protein 0.68 g

Carbohydrate 1.91 g

Total fat 1.57 g

200 ml (7 fl oz/⁷⁄₈ cup) water
10 tbsp honey
6 tbsp soy sauce
4 tbsp roasted grated coconut
3 tbsp roasted ground almonds
2 tbsp peeled and chopped galangal
2 tbsp peeled and chopped ginger
2 tbsp grated palm sugar
1 tbsp shrimp paste

SAUCE

To prepare sauce, mix all ingredients together in a heavy-based saucepan and bring to a boil. Reduce the heat and simmer for about 10 minutes. Skim as necessary. Remove from heat and allow to cool and the sauce will thicken.

20 betel (wild pepper) leaves, or
lettuce leaves, soaked in
water to clean, then dried
6 tbsp roasted grated coconut
6 tbsp peeled and finely diced ginger
6 tbsp finely diced unpeeled lime
4 tbsp chopped roasted almonds
4 tbsp diced shallot
2 tbsp chopped chillies

BETEL LEAF WRAPS

Make a small cup with the betel leaf, place a little of each ingredient inside and drizzle 1 tsp sauce over to taste.

CHICKEN SATAY
SATAY GAI

Makes 15 skewers

150 ml (5 fl oz/⅔ cup) rice vinegar
8 tbsp honey
180 g (6 oz) cucumber, peeled, seeded and sliced
3 tbsp chopped coriander
2 tbsp diagonally sliced red chillies

CUCUMBER RELISH

In a saucepan, bring vinegar and honey to a boil. Stir frequently until honey has dissolved and continue to cook for 15 minutes. Remove from heat, once cooled add cucumber, coriander and chilli, and stir.

NUTRIENTS PER SKEWER

Energy 39.63 kcal
Protein 4.83 g
Carbohydrate 2.05 g
Total fat 1.33 g

1 tbsp red curry paste (see Basics)
100 ml (3½ fl oz/½ cup) coconut milk
200 ml (7 fl oz/⅞ cup) water
50 g (1¾ oz) roasted ground almonds
2½ tbsp soy sauce
2 tbsp tamarind juice (see Basics)
1½ tbsp grated palm sugar

ALMOND SAUCE

In a saucepan, stir-fry red curry paste with half of the coconut milk until fragrant. Add alll remaining ingredients and stir. Simmer on a low to medium heat, stirring frequently, until the mixture is reduced by half.

300 g (10½ oz) chicken breast, skinned and sliced into thin strips
100 ml (3½ fl oz/½ cup) coconut milk
1⅔ tbsp honey
1⅓ tbsp soy sauce
4 coriander roots, minced
3 garlic cloves, minced
¼ tsp ground turmeric
¼ tsp curry powder

CHICKEN SATAY

In a large mixing bowl, combine all ingredients and allow chicken to marinate for 2 hours. Skewer 20 g (¾ oz) of chicken on 15 wooden sticks. Grill satay until cooked. Serve warm with cucumber relish and almond sauce on the side.

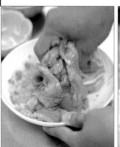

CHEF'S TIP

After marinating, skewer the chicken pieces in a broad 'sewing' fashion and push the pieces together. This ensures that the cooked chicken is moist and succulent.

GRILLED PRAWN RELISH WITH CRUDITÉS
SRAENG WAA

Serves 4

NUTRIENTS PER SERVING
Energy 92.76 kcal
Protein 7.21 g
Carbohydrate 15.38 g
Total fat 0.43 g

3 tbsp soy sauce
2 tbsp roasted chilli paste (see Basics),
discard oil before use
2 tbsp tamarind juice (see Basics)
1½ tbsp lime juice
1½ tbsp grated palm sugar

DRESSING
Place soy sauce, chilli paste, tamarind juice, lime juice and palm sugar in a saucepan, simmer on a medium-low heat and whisk until palm sugar has completely dissolved. Set aside and wait for 15 minutes to allow the flavour to develop.

2 tbsp soy sauce
1 tbsp honey
8 prawns (15 g (½ oz) each), peeled and
de-veined
4 tbsp sliced shallots
2 tbsp finely diagonally sliced lemongrass
3 tbsp peeled and sliced ginger
2 tbsp sliced spring onions
2 kaffir lime leaves, shredded
20 string beans, cut into sticks
15 pieces of baby corn, halved
and boiled for 1 minute
15 peeled carrot sticks
15 seeded cucumber sticks
15 Thai aubergines
15 cherry tomatoes
10 bite-size pieces fresh turmeric

GRILLED PRAWN RELISH
Preheat the grill to a medium heat. Mix soy sauce with the honey in a small bowl or jug and stir until honey has completely dissolved. Place the prawns in a grill pan. Brush generously with soy sauce and honey mixture and grill for 3–4 minutes until prawns are cooked through. Turn the prawns over frequently and baste with the soy sauce and honey mixture while grilling. In a mixing bowl, gently toss the grilled prawns in the dressing with shallots, lemongrass, ginger, spring onions and kaffir lime leaf then transfer mixture into a serving bowl. On a serving plate, place the bowl in the centre and arrange string beans, baby corn, carrot sticks, cucumber sticks, Thai aubergines, cherry tomatoes and pieces of fresh turmeric around and serve.

SPICY CRABMEAT AND KAFFIR LIME BOATS
PLAA POO

Makes 12 pieces

NUTRIENTS PER PIECE

Energy 25.09 kcal

Protein 1.5 g

Carbohydrate 4.72 g

Total fat 0.18 g

2½ tbsp light soy sauce
2 tbsp honey
1½ tbsp lime juice
1 tbsp kaffir lime juice (if unavailable use another tbsp lime juice)
2 bird's eye chillies, finely chopped
65 g (2¼ oz) crabmeat
3 stalks Chinese celery
3 slices ginger
6 tbsp sliced shallots
3 tbsp sliced spring onions
3 tbsp Thai long parsley
2 tbsp finely diagonally sliced lemongrass
2 kaffir lime leaves, shredded
6 small cucumbers, halved lengthways
12 sprigs dill, to garnish
12 mint leaves, to garnish
1 tbsp seeded and sliced sliced red chilli, to garnish

To prepare dressing, combine soy sauce, honey, lime juice, kaffir lime juice and chillies in a bowl and set aside to rest for 2 minutes. To prepare crabmeat, steam with Chinese celery and ginger for 8 minutes. Shred crabmeat and add to the dressing. Sprinkle with shallots, spring onions, Thai long parsley, lemongrass and kaffir lime leaves then toss carefully. To prepare boats, using a teaspoon scrape out the seeds of the cucumber halves and stuff wells with the crabmeat mixture. Garnish with dill, mint and red chilli and serve.

Lay each ingredient on the bottom of the saucepan and place the grid on top. Arrange the salmon loosely on the grid so it can fully absorb the flavours. Cover the pan and place over a medium heat for 20 minutes, until the salmon is cooked and golden brown in colour.

CHEF'S TIP

JASMINE TEA SMOKED SALMON
YAM PLA OB

Makes 30 pieces

NUTRIENTS PER PIECE
Energy 19.45 kcal
Protein 1.41 g
Carbohydrate 2.08 g
Total fat 0.7 g

To prepare dressing, whisk lime juice, honey, lime peel, soy sauce and spring onions in a bowl until well mixed. Set aside. In a saucepan, layer brown rice, brown sugar, jasmine tea leaves, cinnamon sticks, star anise and cloves in that order. Place a grid about 1 cm (½ inch) above the laid ingredients and lay the salmon on the grid. Cover the pan and place over a medium heat for 20 minutes, or until the salmon turns golden brown. In a salad bowl, mix coriander, Thai basil, Thai long parsley, dill, shallots and tomatoes. Shred salmon into mixed herbs and gently toss. Spoon mixture onto cabbage leaves, drizzle lime dressing over and serve.

4 tbsp lime juice
2 tbsp honey
2 tbsp chopped lime peel
2 tbsp soy sauce
4 tbsp chopped spring onions
360 g (12½ oz/1¾ cup) uncooked brown jasmine rice
20 g (⅔ oz) brown sugar
6 g (¼ oz) dried jasmine tea leaves
2 cinnamon sticks
3 pieces star anise
10 cloves
150 g (5½ oz) salmon fillet
4 tbsp coriander leaves
4 tbsp Thai basil leaves
4 tbsp Thai long parsley, sliced
6 sprigs dill leaves
3 tbsp sliced shallots
15 cherry tomatoes, halved
30 Chinese baby cabbage leaves (alternatively, use romaine or butterhead lettuce or endive)

SALMON FISH CAKES
TOD MON PLA

Makes 12 pieces

NUTRIENTS PER PIECE
Energy 100.46 kcal
Protein 10.3 g
Carbohydrate 1.52 g
Total fat 5.62 g

300 g (10½ oz) red pepper, grilled,
peeled, seeded and chopped
5 coriander roots
4 garlic cloves
3 tbsp honey
2 tbsp soy sauce
2 tbsp tamarind juice (see Basics)

SWEET CHILLI SAUCE

Blend all ingredients in a blender. Transfer the mixture to a saucepan. Simmer and stir frequently until sauce consistency is reached. Remove from heat and allow to cool.

250 g (9 oz) salmon fillet, minced
250 g (9 oz) salmon fillet, poached
in boiling water for 5–6 minutes
and flaked
4 tbsp finely sliced basil
4 tbsp finely sliced coriander
4 tbsp chopped spring onions
3½ tbsp roasted ground rice
(see page 43)
3 tbsp soy sauce
2 tbsp finely sliced mint
2 tbsp soy sauce
2 egg whites
1 tsp ground white pepper

FISH CAKES

In a large mixing bowl, combine all ingredients. Divide the mixture into 50 g (1¾ oz) balls and form into cakes. Steam fish cakes for 5 minutes or until they become firm. Heat a non-stick pan and pan-fry fish cakes on each side until golden brown. Serve with sweet chilli sauce on the side.

VEGETABLE ROLLS
KUAY TIEW LOD

Makes 12 pieces

NUTRIENTS PER PIECE

Energy 61.89 kcal

Protein 3.41 g

Carbohydrate 12.41 g

Total fat 0.26 g

SWEET AND SOUR CHILLI SAUCE

Combine all ingredients in a saucepan and simmer on a low heat, stirring frequently. Continue until mixture has reduced by half. Remove from heat and allow to cool.

5 tbsp white wine vinegar
3 tbsp balsamic vinegar
3 tbsp honey
3 tbsp diced red pepper
2 tbsp soy sauce

VEGETABLE ROLLS

In a heated wok, stir-fry garlic using most of the vegetable stock. Add minced chicken, stirring constantly to prevent it from sticking. Then add tofu, bean sprouts and dried shrimp, add more stock to moisten if necessary. Season with soy sauce and honey, and sprinkle with spring onions and ground white pepper. Place the chicken filling and chilli sauce on the mung bean sheets and roll into cylinder shape parcels, similar to a spring roll. Serve with sweet and sour chilli sauce on the side.

2 garlic cloves, chopped
50 ml (2 fl oz/ ¼ cup) vegetable stock (see Basics)
90 g (3¼ oz) chicken breast, minced
40 g (1½ oz) hard tofu, diced
20 g (⅔ oz) bean sprouts, roots removed
15 g (½ oz) dried shrimp
1 tbsp soy sauce
⅔ tbsp honey
4 tbsp chopped spring onions
pinch of ground white pepper
6 mung bean sheets, soaked in water for 10 seconds and halved

CHEF'S TIP | To make smooth egg mixture, beat the eggs and strain through a fine sieve to remove any unwanted lumps. Then add the sliced spring onion.

OMELETTE ROLLS
KHAI YAD SAI

Makes 12 pieces

NUTRIENTS PER PIECE

Energy 76.32 kcal
Protein 8.02 g
Carbohydrate 7.4 g
Total fat 2.76 g

6 eggs, beaten
1 tbsp sliced spring onions
100 ml (3½ fl oz/½ cup) vegetable stock
(see Basics)
4 garlic cloves, finely chopped
9 shallots, sliced
230 g (8 oz) chicken breast, minced
2 tbsp honey
2 tbsp soy sauce
100 g (3½ oz) tomatoes, seeded and diced
pinch of ground black pepper
4 tbsp chopped coriander

To prepare omelettes, mix beaten eggs with spring onions. In a heated, 20 cm (8 inch) non-stick frying pan, pour in about one twelfth of the egg mixture. Immediately tilt the pan to spread the egg into a thin, even layer over the base. Cook over a medium heat until the omelette is just set and the underside is golden. Repeat until all the mixture is used up; this should make 12 omelettes. To prepare filling, heat vegetable stock in a frying pan, add garlic and shallots and cook over a medium heat, stirring occasionally, until soft. Add chicken and cook for 8 minutes, stirring frequently. Stir in honey, soy sauce and tomatoes, season to taste with pepper and simmer over a low heat until slightly thickened. If necessary add more vegetable stock; the consistency should be similar to Italian Bolognaise sauce. Mix in fresh coriander, remove from heat and set aside. Spoon stuffing onto each omelette and roll into a cylinder, similar to a spring roll, and serve.

Pour egg mixture into a non-stick pan over a low heat and swirl the pan to make a thin egg sheet. Keep an eye on the edge of the omelette; as soon as it becomes pale, flip it and cook the other side.

CHEF'S TIP

SALADS

Used as a relish, an accompaniment, or as a whole meal by itself, the unexpected combinations of ingredients in Thai salads give a unique and refreshing taste. Fruit, both ripe and unripe, vegetables, fresh seafood, meat, leaves and flowers, such as banana blossoms, lotus and rose petals, are commonly used as base ingredients. Dressings are always light and oil-free, piquant with lime, hot with chilli, salty with fish sauce and flavoursome with a variety of fresh herbs. Thai salads are a delicious and simple way of increasing the intake of fruit and vegetables and are highly nutritious with a number of vitamins, minerals, antioxidants, enzymes and proteins. The herbs and spices are a rich source of medicinal benefits.

BANANA BLOSSOM SALAD
YAM HUA PLEE

Serves 4

NUTRIENTS PER SERVING

Energy 90.32 kcal

Protein 8.8 g

Carbohydrate 6.33 g

Total fat 3.56 g

CHEF'S TIP

To prevent the banana blossom from browning, trim the purple edges and set them aside for garnishing; slice across the remaining white core and soak in lime juice water so that the flower retains its whiteness.

2½ tbsp lime juice
2 tbsp soy sauce
1½ tbsp honey
1 tbsp roasted chilli paste (see Basics)
2 bird's eye chillies, finely chopped
130 g (4½ oz) banana blossom, peeled, diagonally sliced and soaked in lime juice water
120 g (4¼ oz) chicken breast, boiled for 10 minutes and shredded
3 tbsp ground roasted almonds, coarsely chopped
2 tbsp sliced shallots
2 tbsp chopped spring onions
1 tbsp finely diagonally sliced lemongrass
3 tbsp roasted coconut flakes, to garnish
tip of coriander, to garnish

To prepare dressing, whisk lime juice, soy sauce, honey, chilli paste and chillies in a large bowl. Set aside. To prepare salad, gently toss all remaining ingredients with all of the dressing in a mixing bowl until evenly mixed. Sprinkle over coconut flakes and coriander and serve.

MUSHROOM SALAD
YAM HED RUAM

Serves 4

NUTRIENTS PER SERVING

Energy 73.22 kcal

Protein 2.59 g

Carbohydrate 16.91 g

Total fat 0.38 g

4 tbsp lime juice

3 tbsp soy sauce

1½ tbsp honey

2 bird's eye chillies, finely chopped

120 g (4¼ oz) shiitake mushrooms

120 g (4¼ oz) straw mushrooms

120 g (4¼ oz) wood ear mushrooms, trimmed

6 tbsp sliced spring onions

4 tbsp finely diagonally sliced lemongrass

3 kaffir lime leaves, shredded

To prepare dressing, whisk 3 tbsp of lime juice, soy sauce, honey and chilli in a large bowl until well-mixed. Set aside. Bring 1 L (1¾ pints/4¼ cups) of water to a boil with remaining 1 tbsp of lime juice. Boil shiitake and straw mushrooms for 3 minutes, and wood ear mushrooms for 2 minutes. Drain immediately. Combine all ingredients with dressing in a bowl and gently toss until evenly mixed.

GREEN MANGO AND BEAN CURD SALAD
YAM MA MUANG

Serves 4

NUTRIENTS PER SERVING

Energy 110.66 kcal

Protein 4.9 g

Carbohydrate 17.91 g

Total fat 3.19 g

3 tbsp soy sauce

1½ tbsp honey

1½ tbsp lime juice

2 bird's eye chillies, finely chopped

150 g (5½ oz) green mango, peeled and julienned

120 g (4¼ oz) hard tofu, grilled and cut into strips

2 shallots, finely sliced

6 tbsp chopped coriander

6 tbsp sliced spring onions

2 tbsp finely sliced green and red chillies

2 tbsp finely sliced lemongrass (using only the soft 'heart')

To prepare dressing, whisk soy sauce, honey, lime juice and chillies in a bowl until well mixed. Add all remaining salad ingredients to the bowl with the dressing. Gently toss until evenly mixed.

THAI FRESH FRUIT SALAD
SOM TAM POLLAMAI

Serves 4

NUTRIENTS PER SERVING

Energy 97.96 kcal

Protein 2.94 g

Carbohydrate 14.57 g

Total fat 3.78 g

Fresh and crunchy with a mild fragrant flavour, the rose apple is a small pinkish-red, pear-shaped fruit. Although a juicy thirst-quencher, it does not have much flavour of its own and is mainly used in dishes to absorb and complement other flavours. Traditionally in Indochina it is used to make a cooling drink, administered for fevers.

ROSE APPLE

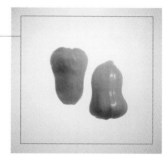

4 tbsp fresh orange juice
2 tbsp lime juice
2 tbsp soy sauce
½ tbsp honey
2 cloves garlic, chopped
2 bird's eye chillies, chopped
120 g (4¼ oz) red apple, diced
120 g (4¼ oz) rose apple, diced
100 g (3½ oz) green apple, diced
60 g (2¼ oz) cherry tomatoes, seeded and sliced
60 g (2¼ oz) guava, diced
40 g (1½ oz) grapes, halved lengthways
40 g (1½ oz) string beans, cut into
2.5 cm (1 inch) lengths and crushed
80 g (2⅔ oz) green mango, julienned
30 g (1 oz) carrot, julienned
8 tbsp roasted ground almonds

To prepare dressing, mix orange juice, lime juice, soy sauce, honey, garlic and chillies in a large bowl. Add red apple, rose apple, and green apple, cherry tomatoes, guava, grapes and string beans to the dressing. Mix well, then add green mango and carrot. Sprinkle with roasted ground almonds and serve.

PRAWN AND POMELO SALAD
YAM SOM O

Serves 4

NUTRIENTS PER SERVING

Energy 98.72 kcal

Protein 6.7 g

Carbohydrate 16.82 g

Total fat 0.88 g

CHEF'S TIP To peel a pomelo, slice off the top and bottom of the green peel, about 3–5 cm (1–2 inch), and carefully, using a knife or your fingers, peel off the white pith which has a bitter taste. Break the peeled pomelo in half and separate into individual wedges. For the salad, shred each wedge to separate the small juice sacs.

3 tbsp lime juice
2½ tbsp soy sauce
1½ tbsp honey
2 bird's eye chillies, finely chopped
300 g (10½ oz) pomelo, peeled and each segment shredded
120 g (4¼ oz) prawn, peeled, de-veined and boiled
60 g (2¼ oz) tomatoes, diced
2 shallots, finely sliced
4 tbsp sliced spring onions
2 tbsp finely sliced lemongrass (using only the soft 'heart')
4 tbsp roasted coconut flakes, to garnish

To prepare dressing, combine lime juice, soy sauce, honey and chillies in a bowl and whisk well. Set aside. In a mixing bowl, gently toss all remaining salad ingredients with dressing until well mixed. Sprinkle roasted coconut flakes over and serve.

WINGED BEAN AND SCALLOP SALAD
YAM THUA PLU

Serves 4

NUTRIENTS PER SERVING
Energy 161.31 kcal
Protein 10.41 g
Carbohydrate 9.38 g
Total fat 9.11 g

2½ tbsp lime juice
2½ tbsp soy sauce
2 tbsp roasted chilli paste (see Basics)
1½ tbsp honey
2 bird's eye chillies, finely chopped
300 g (10½ oz) winged beans
160 g (5¾ oz) scallops, cooked
3 medium shallots, finely sliced
4 tbsp sliced spring onions
1 hard boiled egg, cut into 6 wedges, to garnish
3 tbsp roasted coconut flakes, to garnish

To prepare the dressing, combine lime juice, soy sauce, chilli paste, honey and chillies in a bowl and whisk well. To prepare salad, blanch winged beans in boiling water for 1 minute, transfer to iced water and drain so that the beans stay crunchy. In a mixing bowl, gently toss all salad ingredients with dressing until well mixed. Garnish with boiled egg and coconut flakes and serve.

The winged bean is also known as asparagus pea, Goa bean, or princess pea. It is referred to as a 'one species supermarket' as the whole plant is edible. The green pods are very decorative, with four serrated edges or 'wings' and are mainly served in salads. They are nutty in flavour and provide a good source of protein, vitamin A and other vitamins.

WINGED BEAN

SPICED MINCED CHICKEN SALAD
LAAB GAI

Serves 4

NUTRIENTS PER SERVING
Energy 165.14 kcal
Protein 21.52 g
Carbohydrate 16.23 g
Total fat 1.53 g

350 g (12 oz) chicken breast, minced
2 tbsp vegetable stock (see Basics)
4 tbsp lime juice
3 tbsp soy sauce
1 tbsp honey
4 tbsp roasted ground rice (see below)
3 tsp chilli powder
4 shallots, sliced into rings
20 g (¾ oz) spring onions, chopped
8 tbsp chopped coriander
8 tbsp chopped Thai long parsley
4 tbsp chopped mint
tip of purple basil to garnish

In a saucepan, stir-fry minced chicken with vegetable stock for 3–4 minutes or until cooked. Set aside. Combine lime juice, soy sauce and honey, add cooked minced chicken with juice, ground rice and chilli powder and mix well. Sprinkle with sliced shallots, spring onions, coriander, Thai long parsley and mint. Garnish with tip of purple basil and serve.

ROASTED GROUND RICE

In a heavy-based frying pan, toss 150 g (5½ oz) uncooked jasmine rice, 3–4 kaffir lime leaves and 2 thin slices galangal over a medium heat until the rice turns golden brown in colour. Place the rice in a blender and blend to a fine powder.

CHEF'S TIP | Roasted ground rice can be kept in an airtight jar at room temperature for at least one month. Roasted ground rice is also used in Salmon Fish Cakes (page 26) and Grilled Beef Salad (page 46).

CHICKEN SALAD WITH SPICY HERB DRESSING
YAM TAWAI

Serves 4

NUTRIENTS PER SERVING

Energy 84.14 kcal

Protein 8.83 g

Carbohydrate 10.57 g

Total fat 0.76 g

1 tbsp Massaman curry paste (see Basics)

2 tbsp soy sauce

2 tbsp tamarind juice (see Basics)

1 tbsp honey

100 g (3½ oz) bok choy leaves, trimmed

80 g (2⅔ oz) baby corn, cut diagonally into bite-size pieces

80 g (2⅔ oz) bean sprouts

1 L (1¾ pints/4¼ cups) soy milk

100 g (3½ oz) chicken breast, boiled for 8 minutes and sliced

1 chilli, finely sliced, to garnish

To prepare spicy herb dressing, stir-fry Massaman curry paste until fragrant. Add soy sauce, tamarind juice and honey and whisk until well mixed. Set aside. Blanch bok choy, baby corn and bean sprouts in separate pans of boiling soy milk for 1–2 minutes. Place chicken slices in a mixing bowl with dressing and vegetables and gently toss until well mixed. Sprinkle over sliced chilli and serve.

GLASS NOODLE SALAD
YAM WUN SEN

Serves 4

NUTRIENTS PER SERVING
Energy 103.99 kcal
Protein 6.04 g
Carbohydrate 20.25 g
Total fat 0.18 g

3 garlic cloves
2 bird's eye chillies, chopped
4 tbsp fresh lime juice
3 tbsp soy sauce
1½ tbsp honey
180 g (6 oz) glass noodles, soaked in water until soft
2½ tbsp julienned carrot
50 g (1¾ oz) wood ear mushrooms, trimmed
120 g (4¼ oz) prawns, peeled, de-veined and cooked
50 g (1¾ oz) tomatoes, seeded and sliced
½ onion, sliced
4 tbsp chopped Chinese celery
2 tbsp chopped coriander
2 tbsp chopped spring onions

To prepare dressing, blend garlic, chillies, lime juice, soy sauce and honey in a food processor until well mixed. Set aside. Plunge noodles, carrot and wood ear mushrooms in 1 L (1¾ pints/4¼ cups) of boiling water for about 30 seconds and drain. Place the noodles, carrot and wood ear mushrooms in a mixing bowl, add cooked prawns, tomatoes, onion, Chinese celery, coriander, spring onions and dressing. Toss the salad well, transfer to serving bowls and serve immediately.

SPICED GRILLED BEEF SALAD WITH SIAMESE HERBS

YAM NEAU YANG

Serves 4

NUTRIENTS PER SERVING
Energy 181.17 kcal
Protein 21.84 g
Carbohydrate 6.26 g
Total fat 7.22 g

2 garlic cloves
3 mint stems, chopped
3 bird's eye chillies
4 tbsp lime juice
3 tbsp soy sauce
4 tbsp honey
1 tbsp roasted ground rice (see page 43)
2 (200 g (7 oz) each) grilled beef fillets,
sliced into bite-size pieces (see opposite)
6 tbsp finely sliced shallots
4 tbsp finely diagonally sliced lemongrass
4 tbsp fresh mint leaves
pinch of finely sliced kaffir lime leaves
pinch of seeded and finely sliced red chilli

Using a pestle and mortar, pound garlic, mint stems and chillies together until a paste is formed. Transfer paste to a mixing bowl. Add lime juice, soy sauce, honey and ground rice to create a spicy and tangy mint dressing. On a serving plate, place prepared beef fillet in the centre and arrange remaining ingredients on top. Pour over dressing and serve.

GRILLED BEEF

Marinate the beef in 2 tbsp soy sauce and a pinch of ground pepper for 10 minutes, then grill the beef until medium-well done. Slice into bite-size pieces.

SOUPS

In Thailand, soups are usually served with the main meal. They are used to provide harmony between spicy, mild, salty, sweet, bitter and sour flavours and to balance a meal that contains drier ingredients. Chiva-Som's soups blend traditional ingredients with the spa cuisine principles and these recipes respectfully adapt old methods to provide lighter and healthier alternatives without compromising flavour and balance.

SEAFOOD SOUP WITH HOLY BASIL
POH-TAK

Serves 4

NUTRIENTS PER SERVING
Energy 114.23 kcal
Protein 15.99 g
Carbohydrate 10.82 g
Total fat 1.4 g

Trawled from the Gulf of Thailand, adjacent to Chiva-Som, fresh tiger prawns are a popular item on the menu. Although the fat content is quite low, the cholesterol level is high, so these are great for an occasional treat.

PRAWN

1 L (1¾ pints/4¼ cups) vegetable stock (see Basics)
4 tbsp finely sliced galangal
4 tbsp finely sliced lemongrass
4 kaffir lime leaves, finely sliced
4 bird's eye chillies, crushed
90 g (3¼ oz) prawns, peeled and de-veined
90 g (3¼ oz) red snapper fillet, cut into bite-size pieces
90 g (3¼ oz) scallops
60 g (2¼ oz) squid, sliced into 1 cm (½ inch) thick rings
4 fresh mussels, cleaned
4 sea crab claws
90 g (3¼ oz) straw mushrooms, trimmed and halved
60 g (2¼ oz) cherry tomatoes, sliced
4 tbsp miso paste
3½ tbsp lime juice
6 tbsp holy basil
3 tbsp sliced Thai long parsley
2 roasted dried red chillies, sliced

In a saucepan, bring vegetable stock to a boil with galangal, lemongrass, kaffir lime leaves and chillies. Boil for several minutes until the flavours are infused. Add prawns, red snapper, scallops, squid, mussels, sea crab claws, mushrooms and cherry tomatoes. Add each ingredient one at a time and boil for 4–5 minutes until cooked. Once cooked, remove from heat and add miso paste and lime juice. Sprinkle with holy basil, Thai long parsley and roasted dried red chillies and serve.

HERBED MUSHROOM COCONUT SOUP
TOM KHA HED

Serves 4

NUTRIENTS PER SERVING

Energy 139.81 kcal

Protein 3.39 g

Carbohydrate 12.19 g

Total fat 10.07 g

In a saucepan, bring vegetable stock and coconut milk to a boil. Add galangal, lemongrass, kaffir lime leaves, chillies and simmer for several minutes until the flavours are infused. Then add all mushrooms and cook for 4–5 minutes. Remove from heat and season with miso paste and lime juice. Garnish with kaffir lime leaf and coriander leaf and serve.

400 ml (14 fl oz/1⅔ cups) vegetable stock (see Basics)

200 ml (7 fl oz/⅞ cup) coconut milk

3 tbsp peeled and julienned galangal

3 tbsp finely diagonally sliced lemongrass

2 kaffir lime leaves, finely sliced

3 bird's eye chillies, crushed

80 g (2⅔ oz) straw mushrooms

60 g (2¼ oz) oyster mushrooms, trimmed

60 g (2¼ oz) shiitake mushrooms, trimmed

60 g (2¼ oz) wood ear mushrooms, trimmed

4 tbsp miso paste

2 tbsp lime juice

pinch of shredded kaffir lime leaves, to garnish

tip of coriander leaf, to garnish

HERBED CHICKEN COCONUT SOUP
TOM KHA GAI

Serves 4

400 ml (14 fl oz/1⅔ cups) vegetable stock (see Basics)
200 ml (7 fl oz/⅞ cup) coconut milk
3 tbsp peeled and julienned galangal
3 tbsp finely diagonally sliced lemongrass
2 kaffir lime leaves, finely sliced
3 bird's eye chillies, crushed
160 g (5¾ oz) chicken breast, cut into bite-size pieces
30 g (1 oz) oyster mushrooms, trimmed
30 g (1 oz) straw mushrooms, peeled and cut into wedges
15 g (½ oz) cherry tomatoes, halved
4 tbsp miso paste
2 tbsp lime juice
1 tbsp red chilli, seeded and diagonally sliced, to garnish
2 sprigs kaffir lime leaves, to garnish
tip of coriander leaf, to garnish

In a saucepan, bring vegetable stock and coconut milk to a boil. Add galangal, lemongrass, kaffir lime leaves and chillies and simmer for several minutes. Then add chicken, mushrooms and tomatoes and cook for 4–5 minutes until well-done (overcooked chicken will become tough). Remove from heat and season with miso paste and lime juice. Garnish with red chilli slices, kaffir lime leaves and coriander and serve.

NUTRIENTS PER SERVING

Energy 67.76 kcal
Protein 10.99 g
Carbohydrate 9.93 g
Total fat 10.48 g

STUFFED CUCUMBER SOUP
TOM JUED TAN-KWA YAD SAI

Serves 4

NUTRIENTS PER SERVING
Energy 101.01 kcal
Protein 9.29 g
Carbohydrate 15.21 g
Total fat 0.64 g

140 g (5 oz) chicken breast, minced
40 g (1½ oz) glass noodles, soaked in water,
cut into 7.5 cm (3 inch) lengths
2 coriander roots, finely chopped
2 garlic cloves, finely chopped
¾ tbsp soy sauce
pinch of ground white pepper
4 long cucumbers, peeled, halved and cored

CUCUMBER STUFFING
Marinate minced chicken and glass noodles with coriander root, garlic, soy sauce and ground white pepper. Stuff the mixture into the 8 cucumber cores.

1 L (1¾ pints/4¼ cups) vegetable stock (see Basics)
8 stuffed cucumber halves
80 g (2⅔ oz) shiitake mushrooms
1½ tbsp soy sauce
pinch of ground white pepper
2 tbsp sliced spring onions, to garnish

STUFFED CUCUMBER SOUP
In a saucepan, bring vegetable stock to a boil and add stuffed cucumber and mushrooms. Increase the heat and boil for 5–8 minutes, until chicken is cooked. Skim the soup as necessary. Remove from heat and season with soy sauce and ground pepper. Sprinkle with spring onions and serve.

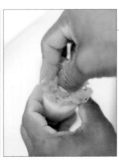

CHEF'S TIP Peel the cucumber and cut into 5-cm-long (2 inch) cylinders. Core the cucumber and, using your fingers, stuff the marinated chicken mixture inside each cucumber.

SPICED AND SOUR PRAWN SOUP

TOM YAM GOONG

Serves 4

600 ml (1 pint/2 cups) vegetable stock (see Basics)
3 medium shallots, quartered and crushed
3 tbsp julienned galangal
3 tbsp finely diagonally sliced lemongrass
3 kaffir lime leaves, finely sliced
3 bird's eye chillies, crushed
90 g (3¼ oz) straw mushrooms, trimmed and halved
30 g (1 oz) cherry tomatoes, halved
8 prawns (15 g (½ oz) each) peeled and de-veined
4 tbsp miso paste
3 tbsp lime juice
1 tbsp apple concentrate or honey

In a saucepan, place vegetable stock, shallots, galangal, lemongrass, kaffir lime leaves and chillies and bring to a boil for 4–5 minutes. Then add straw mushrooms, cherry tomatoes and prawns. Once cooked, remove from heat and season with miso paste, lime juice and apple concentrate.

NUTRIENTS PER SERVING

Energy 81.11 kcal
Protein 9.63 g
Carbohydrate 11.03 g
Total fat 0.62 g

SPICED AND SOUR MUSHROOM SOUP

TOM YAM HED

Serves 4

600 ml (1 pint/2 cups) vegetable stock (see Basics)
3 medium shallots, quartered and crushed
3 tbsp julienned galangal
3 tbsp finely diagonally sliced lemongrass
3 kaffir lime leaves, finely sliced
3 bird's eye chillies, pressed
90 g (3¼ oz) oyster mushrooms, sliced
90 g (3¼ oz) straw mushrooms, trimmed and halved
60 g (2¼ oz) cherry tomatoes, halved
4 tbsp miso paste
3 tbsp lime juice
1 tbsp apple concentrate or honey

In a saucepan, bring vegetable stock, shallots, galangal, lemongrass, kaffir lime leaves and chillies to a boil. Continue to boil for 4–5 minutes. Add oyster and straw mushrooms and cherry tomatoes. Once cooked remove from heat and season with miso paste, lime juice and apple concentrate.

NUTRIENTS PER SERVING

Energy 63.05 kcal
Protein 4.11 g
Carbohydrate 12.63 g
Total fat 0.68 g

CURRIES

Stimulating the senses with exotic aromas and tastes, curries reflect the botanical and cultural diversity of different spices, herbs and cooking methods from the whole of Asia. Generally, curry refers to a blend of various spices but the word is a Tamil term meaning sauce. This would imply a dish with a fairly liquid consistency which may not necessarily be spicy. The spices used in curries all have diverse medicinal qualities. They commonly assist the digestive function and have an anti-inflammatory effect. Therapeutically, different spices such as turmeric, ginger and cinnamon are used in large doses by both Western and Eastern herbalists to treat a variety of ailments.

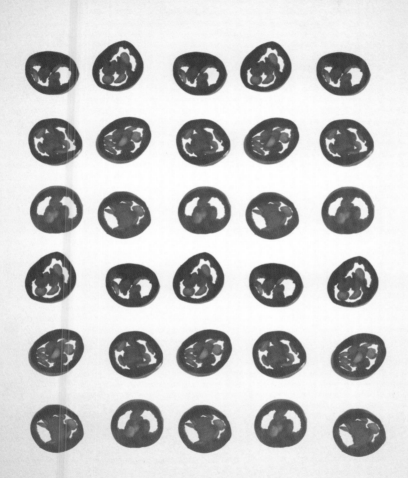

ROCK LOBSTER CURRY
GAENG KAREE KUNG

Serves 4

NUTRIENTS PER SERVING

Energy 438.37 kcal

Protein 23.58 g

Carbohydrate 54.53 g

Total fat 16.25 g

CHEF'S TIP

Plunge the live lobster in boiling water for 15 seconds and allow to cool. Twist off the claws. Using kitchen scissors, cut between the head and tail fan and twist off the head. On the underside of the tail fan, cut along the centre of the soft membrane, detach the hard protective membrane and take out the tail meat in a single piece.

6 dried red chillies, seeded and
soaked in water until soft
2 cm (1 inch) piece galangal, peeled and sliced
½ tsp coriander seeds
½ tsp cumin seeds
1 tsp ground cinnamon
1 tsp ground turmeric
4 cardamom pods
4 cloves
2 medium shallots
3 garlic cloves

CURRY PASTE

Using a pestle and mortar, gradually add each ingredient in the order listed, pound each ingredient from hard and dried to soft and wet before adding the next. Or, using a blender, add little by little of each ingredient. To soften, add a little water or soy sauce. Blend until puréed.

250 ml (9 fl oz/1 cup) coconut milk
80 ml (2½ fl oz/⅓ cup) curry paste
10 tbsp miso paste
40 g (1½ oz) grated palm sugar
2 tbsp tamarind juice (see Basics)
1 L (1¾ pints/4¼ cups) vegetable stock (see Basics)
400 g (14 oz) potatoes, cut into 2 cm (1 inch) cubes
and boiled for 8 minutes
200 g (7 oz) onion, cut into 2 cm (1 inch) cubes
320 g (11½ oz) rock lobster, shelled and sliced
80 g (2⅔ oz) shallots, quartered, to garnish
2 tbsp sliced red chillies, to garnish
2 tbsp sliced and toasted shallots, to garnish

ROCK LOBSTER CURRY

Pour half the coconut milk into a large heavy-based pan over a medium heat and bring to a boil, stirring constantly. Stir in curry paste and cook for 2–3 minutes until mixture is fragrant and thoroughly blended. Add miso paste and palm sugar and mix well. Add tamarind juice, vegetable stock and remaining coconut milk and bring back to a boil. Then add cooked potato and onion, reduce the heat and simmer for several minutes. Add rock lobster and cook for 3–4 minutes. Remove from heat. Garnish with shallot quarters, red chillies and toasted shallots and serve.

LAMB GREEN CURRY
GAENG KIAW WAN KAE

Serves 4

NUTRIENTS PER SERVING

Energy 347.21 kcal

Protein 24.98 g

Carbohydrate 20.76 g

Total fat 19.29 g

250 ml (9 fl oz/1 cup) coconut milk

3½ tbsp green curry paste (see Basics)

6½ tbsp miso paste

2 tbsp honey

1 L (1¾ pints/4¼ cups) vegetable stock (see Basics)

300 g (10½ oz) Thai aubergine, cut into wedges

120 g (4¼ oz) Thai pea aubergine

400 g (14 oz) lamb loin, cut into bite-size pieces

2 large red chillies, cut into 2.5 cm (1 inch) lengths

4 kaffir lime leaves, torn

4 handfuls Thai basil leaves, trimmed

In a large heavy pan, place coconut milk over a medium heat and bring to a boil, stirring constantly. Stir in green curry paste and cook for 2–3 minutes until mixture is fragrant and thoroughly blended. Add miso paste and honey and mix well. Gradually add vegetable stock, stirring constantly. Bring back to a boil, add Thai aubergine wedges and Thai pea aubergines, stir constantly for 4–5 minutes or until the aubergines are half done. Add sliced lamb and cook for 2–3 minutes or until the lamb is nearly done. Sprinkle over chillies, kaffir lime leaves and Thai basil. Remove from heat and allow to cool. Serve with brown rice. The lamb can be cooked beforehand by poaching in vegetable stock for 6 minutes or grilled until medium-well done, then sliced.

VEGETABLE GREEN CURRY WITH TOFU
GAENG KIAW WAN JAY

Serves 4

NUTRIENTS PER SERVING
Energy 291.2 kcal
Protein 11.26 g
Carbohydrate 30.13 g
Total fat 16.04 g

250 ml (9 fl oz/1 cup) coconut milk
2 tbsp green curry paste (see Basics)
4 tbsp miso paste
2 tbsp honey
1 L (1¾ pints/4¼ cups) vegetable stock (see Basics)
200 g (7 oz) Thai aubergine, cut into wedges
120 g (4¼ oz) baby corn, sliced
diagonally and boiled for 2 minutes
120 g (4¼ oz) carrots, sliced and boiled for 2 minutes
120 g (4¼ oz) straw mushrooms,
halved and boiled for 2 minutes
320 g (11½ oz) hard tofu, cubed
2 large red and green chillies, sliced
4 kaffir lime leaves, torn
4 handfuls Thai basil leaves

Pour coconut milk into a large heavy-based pan over a medium heat and bring to a boil, stirring constantly. Stir in green curry paste and cook for 2–3 minutes until fragrant and thoroughly blended. Add miso paste and honey and mix well. Gradually add vegetable stock, stirring constantly. Bring back to a boil and add Thai aubergine wedges, stirring constantly for 4–5 minutes or until the aubergine is half done. Then add baby corn, carrots, straw mushrooms and tofu and cook for 2–3 minutes. Sprinkle with chillies, kaffir lime leaves and Thai basil. Remove from heat and allow to cool. Serve with brown rice.

RICH BEEF CURRY
PANAENG NEUA

Serves 4

NUTRIENTS PER SERVING
Energy 271.44 kcal
Protein 24.12 g
Carbohydrate 18.87 g
Total fat 10.99 g

150 ml (5 fl oz/⅔ cup) coconut milk
2 tbsp red curry paste (see Basics)
3 tbsp soy sauce
2 tbsp grated palm sugar
50 g (1¾ oz) lemongrass, bruised
100 ml (3½ fl oz/½ cup) vegetable stock (see Basics)
400 g (14 oz) rump beef steak,
trimmed of fat and cut into thin strips
1 red and 1 green chilli, sliced
pinch of tapioca flour

Pour 100 ml (3½ fl oz/½ cup) coconut milk into a large heavy-based pan over a medium heat and bring to a boil, stirring constantly. Stir in red curry paste and cook for 2–3 minutes until mixture is fragrant and well blended. Add soy sauce, palm sugar and bruised lemongrass. Mix well. Continue to cook until the colour deepens. Gradually add vegetable stock, stirring constantly. Bring back to a boil and add beef strips. Cook, stirring constantly, for 15–20 minutes or until the liquid has reduced by a third. Add chillies, remove from heat and allow to cool. (The chillies could be added after the curry has cooled to prevent the colour from changing.) Once cooled, remove lemongrass and keep in a cool place. To prepare thickened coconut milk, boil remaining 50 ml (2 fl oz/¼ cup) coconut milk with tapioca flour and simmer until mixture has reduced by half. Place beef curry on serving plates and pour over thickened coconut milk. Serve with brown rice.

RED CURRY PASTE

Using a pestle and mortar, pound the chilli first, followed by galangal, lemongrass, kaffir lime zest, coriander root, cumin seeds, shallot, garlic and shrimp paste. The ingredients must be added in that order. Before adding each ingredient, ensure that the previous has been mashed until smooth.

RED DUCK CURRY
GAENG PET PED YANG

Serves 4

NUTRIENTS PER SERVING

Energy 425.43 kcal

Protein 22.69 g

Carbohydrate 41.5 g

Total fat 9.3 g

KAFFIR LIME LEAF

The fragrant leaves of kaffir limes are used to give incomparable flavour to certain Thai dishes. The leaves, when young and tender, are finely shredded and added to salads and can also be sprinkled over curries for a burst of flavour. They have a distinct perfume and are indispensable in the tangy soups, salads and curries that are an essential part of traditional Thai cuisine.

300 ml (10 fl oz/1¼ cup) coconut milk
4 tbsp red curry paste (see Basics)
140 g (5 oz) dried Chinese dates, seeded and soaked
3 tbsp grated palm sugar
6 tbsp miso paste
1 L (1¾ pints/4¼ cups) vegetable stock (see Basics)
320 g (11½ oz) skinned duck breast, cut into bite-size pieces
140 g (5 oz) cherry tomatoes
3 tbsp sliced red and green chillies
3 kaffir lime leaves, finely sliced
2 handfuls Thai basil leaves
pinch of tapioca flour

Pour 250 ml (9 fl oz/1 cup) coconut milk into a large heavy-based pan over a medium heat and bring to a boil. Stir in red curry paste and simmer for several minutes. Add dried Chinese dates, palm sugar and miso paste. Gradually add vegetable stock, stirring constantly. Then add duck breast and cook for 8–10 minutes until done. Add cherry tomatoes and bring back to a boil. Add chillies and kaffir lime leaves. Remove from heat. To prepare thickened coconut milk, boil remaining 50 ml (2 fl oz/¼ cup) coconut milk with tapioca flour and simmer until mixture has reduced by half. Place duck curry on serving plates and pour over 2 tbsp thickened coconut milk on each plate. Serve with brown rice.

SOUTHERN THAI-STYLE CHICKEN CURRY
MASSAMAN GAI

Serves 4

NUTRIENTS PER SERVING
Energy 299.13 kcal
Protein 23.86 g
Carbohydrate 31.78 g
Total fat 9.1 g

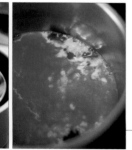

CHEF'S TIP | Break up the tamarind by hand and soak for 5 minutes in warm water. Once softened, squeeze and knead the pulp to obtain maximum flavour. Sieve the juice and discard the remaining pulp.

100 ml (3½ fl oz/½ cup) coconut milk
4 tbsp massaman curry paste (see Basics)
5 tbsp miso paste
2 tbsp grated palm sugar
650 ml (1 pint/2¾ cups) vegetable stock (see Basics)
2 tbsp tamarind juice (see Basics)
320 g (11½ oz) skinless chicken breast, cubed
200 g (7 oz) potato, peeled and cubed
100 g (3½ oz) onion, peeled and cubed
2 cinnamon sticks
5 pieces star anise
5 cardamom pods

Pour half of the coconut milk into a large heavy-based pan over a medium heat and bring to a boil, stirring constantly. Stir in massaman curry paste and cook for 2–3 minutes until mixture is fragrant and thoroughly blended. Add miso paste and palm sugar, mix well. Add vegetable stock, tamarind juice and remaining coconut milk and bring back to a boil. Add chicken, potato and onion, reduce the heat and simmer. Continue cooking. Once tender, remove chicken and potato and keep separate. Simmer until sauce thickens, then return chicken and potato to the pan, bring to a boil for 4–5 minutes. Serve with brown rice.

YELLOW KING FISH CURRY
GAENG LUANG PLA IN-SEE

Serves 4

NUTRIENTS PER SERVING
Energy 266.46 kcal
Protein 30.36 g
Carbohydrate 25.6 g
Total fat 4.86 g

Large pods of tamarind contain a sour-sweet pulp, which becomes more sour once dried. Often used as a flavouring, it blends well with other sweet tastes. Tamarind is rich in vitamins and minerals and is used to cool the system and cleanse the blood. See Basics for tamarind juice recipe.

TAMARIND

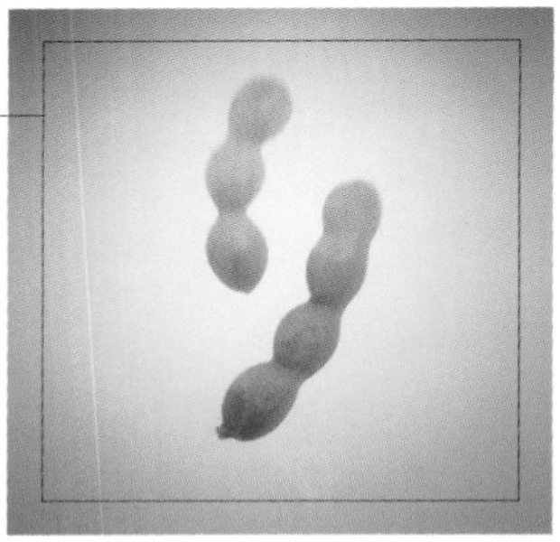

1 L (1¾ pints/4¼ cups) vegetable stock (see Basics)
1 tbsp red curry paste (see Basics)
½ tsp ground turmeric
10 tbsp miso paste
3½ tbsp grated palm sugar
4 tbsp tamarind juice (see Basics)
480 g (1 lb 1 oz) sliced king fish steak
200 g (7 oz) gourd ivy leaves or baby spinach

In a large pan, bring vegetable stock to a boil. Add red curry paste and ground turmeric, stir well. Season with miso paste, palm sugar and tamarind juice. Bring back to a boil and poach king fish steaks in the curry for 8–10 minutes until cooked. Drop gourd ivy leaves in curry and pour into serving bowls. Serve with brown rice.

MAINS

Western culture has modified Thai cooking over time. These creative main dishes return to the 'lighter' Thai tradition with a spa cuisine touch. Fresh local seafood is emphasized, and lamb, beef, chicken and vegetarian dishes also feature. All are seasoned with aromatic and flavoursome Thai herbs. To reduce the 'heaviness' vegetable stock is used in place of oil when stir-frying, and unnecessary amounts of coconut cream have been reduced. The lightness of these main meals complements Chiva-Som nutritionists' recommendations to avoid large heavy meals late at night as our metabolism is higher earlier in the day.

PAN-FRIED POMFRET WITH SWEET CHILLI SAUCE
JARAMED SAM ROD

Serves 4

NUTRIENTS PER SERVING
Energy 188.95 kcal
Protein 24.62 g
Carbohydrate 11.72 g
Total fat 5.36 g

300 ml (10 fl oz/1¼ cups) vegetable stock (see Basics)
120 g (4¼ oz) pineapple, peeled, cored and diced
80 g (2⅔ oz) red pepper, finely chopped
40 g (1½ oz) onion, sliced
3 tbsp miso paste
2 tbsp soy sauce
1½ tbsp honey
1½ tbsp tamarind juice (see Basics)
1 tbsp oyster sauce
4 garlic cloves
3 medium red chillies
3 coriander roots, finely chopped

SWEET CHILLI SAUCE

Blend all ingredients in a food processor, transfer to a small pan and bring to a boil, simmer until mixture has reduced by half.

1 tbsp lime juice
1 tbsp soy sauce
pinch ground white pepper
4 pomfret fillets (120 g (4¼ oz) each)
160 g (5¾ oz) pineapple, diced
3 medium red chillies, cut into 2.5 cm (1 inch) lengths

PAN-FRIED POMFRET

To prepare marinade, combine lime juice, soy sauce and ground white pepper. Heat a heavy-based pan, dip pomfret fillets in marinade and pan-fry each side. Remove from heat and cover to keep warm. Arrange pineapple on each serving plate and place cooked fish on top. Pour over sweet chilli sauce, sprinkle over sliced chilli and serve.

KING FISH WITH FRESH CHILLI PASTE
PLA IN SEE PAD PRIG SOD

Serves 4

NUTRIENTS PER SERVING
Energy 166.1 kcal
Protein 19.64 g
Carbohydrate 15.44 g
Total fat 2.93 g

King fish is a lean fish high in fatty acids and has a firm texture similar to sword fish. King fish is a great source of protein and the omega 3 'good oils' which nourish the nervous system and have anti-inflammatory properties. These good oils also help to decrease cholesterol and blood pressure, as well as decrease blood clotting tendencies.

KING FISH

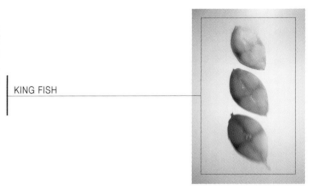

80 g (2²⁄₃ oz) onions, sliced
8 cloves garlic, chopped
300 ml (10 fl oz/1¼ cups) vegetable stock (see Basics)
2 tbsp fresh chilli paste (see Basics)
320 g (11½ oz) king fish fillet, sliced into bite-size pieces
5 tbsp miso paste
1 tbsp honey
1 tbsp oyster sauce
2 red chillies, sliced into 2.5 cm (1 inch) lengths
4 handfuls Thai basil

In a heavy wok, stir-fry onion and garlic over a low–medium heat, gradually adding half of the vegetable stock. Once golden brown, add fresh chilli paste and fry until fragrant. Then add remaining vegetable stock, bring to a boil and add king fish pieces. Cook fish on both sides and season with miso paste, honey and oyster sauce. Sprinkle with sliced red chilli and Thai basil leaves and remove from heat. Serve with brown rice.

CHEF'S TIP

Steam the banana leaf quickly in a steamer before use. This will prevent the leaf from cracking, making it more pliable and easier to wrap the filling.

CURRIED FISH MOUSSE
HOR MOK YANG

Serves 4

In a mixing bowl, mix minced king fish with red curry paste. Once well mixed, add egg whites and coconut milk little by little. Using a wooden spatula, stir constantly in the same direction. Season with soy sauce and honey. Add cubed king fish and mix thoroughly. On each banana leaf, place some cabbage as a base, top with 3 tbsp fish mousse, Thai basil, red chilli and kaffir lime leaf. Wrap banana leaf, fasten with cocktail sticks and steam for 6–8 minutes. Grill each packet for 2–3 minutes, or until well cooked, and serve with brown rice.

200 g (7 oz) minced king fish
2 tbsp red curry paste (see Basics)
3 egg whites
60 ml (2 fl oz/¼ cup) coconut milk
3 tbsp soy sauce
1⅓ tbsp honey
100 g (3½ oz) king fish fillet, cut into 1.5 cm (½ inch) cubes
20 banana leaves, cut 25 x 30 cm (10 x 12 inch), cleaned and dried
60 g (2¼ oz) cabbage, shredded
20 g (⅔ oz) Thai basil
4 red chillies, seeded and sliced
10 kaffir lime leaves, finely sliced

NUTRIENTS PER SERVING
Energy 156.37 kcal
Protein 18.59 g
Carbohydrate 8.86 g
Total fat 5.26 g

GRILLED SEA BASS
PLA KRA PONG YANG BAI TONG

Serves 4

To prepare marinade, combine oyster sauce, soy sauce, garlic, coriander roots, ground black pepper and mix well. Place sea bass in the marinade along with lemongrass and pandan leaves. Leave in the fridge for 10 minutes. Wrap marinated fish in banana leaf, fasten and bake in the oven at 220°C (420°F) for 15 minutes or grill for 15 minutes on each side. Serve with seafood dip.

75 ml (2½ fl oz/⅓ cup) oyster sauce
50 ml (2 fl oz/¼ cup) soy sauce
4 garlic cloves, chopped
10 coriander roots, chopped
1 tsp ground black pepper
4 whole sea bass (600 g (1 lb 5 oz) each), scaled and gutted
3 stalks lemongrass, roughly chopped and crushed
4 pandan leaves, cut into 7.5 cm (3 inch) lengths
8 banana leaves, cut 25 x 30 cm (10 x 12 inch)
3 tbsp seafood dip (see Basics)

NUTRIENTS PER SERVING
Energy 256.9 kcal
Protein 39.5 g
Carbohydrate 14.06 g
Total fat 4.14 g

STEAMED GAROUPA WITH SOY SAUCE AND GINGER BROTH

PLA GAO NUNG KING

Serves 4

NUTRIENTS PER SERVING

Energy 138.67 kcal

Protein 25.32 g

Carbohydrate 7.74 g

Total fat 0.37 g

500 ml (18 fl oz/2¼ cups) water

10 g (¼ oz) bonito flakes
(Japanese dried fish flakes)

30 g (1 oz) fresh ginger,
peeled and cut into chunks

10 g (¼ oz) kombu seaweed

4 tbsp soy sauce

1 tbsp oyster sauce

pinch of ground white pepper

4 garoupa fillets (120 g (4¼ oz) each), skinned

80 g (2⅔ oz) fresh shiitake mushrooms, sliced into discs

40 g (1½ oz) fresh ginger, peeled and sliced into discs

4 garlic cloves, sliced into discs

240 ml (9 fl oz/1 cup) soy and ginger broth

40 g (1½ oz) carrots, shredded, to garnish

20 g (¾ oz) spring onions, shredded, to garnish

4 sprigs dill, to garnish

SOY SAUCE AND GINGER BROTH

In a large saucepan, bring water to a boil. Stir in bonito flakes, ginger and kombu seaweed. Reduce the heat to simmer and continue cooking for 15–20 minutes or until the water has reduced by four-fifths. Once reduced, discard bonito flakes, ginger and kombu, using a sieve if necessary, and bring liquid back to a boil. Season with soy sauce, oyster sauce and ground pepper. Cook for 3–4 minutes. Remove from heat and set aside.

STEAMED FISH

On a steaming tray, arrange garoupa fillets neatly in rows. Place sliced shiitake mushrooms (leaving some for garnishing), ginger and garlic on each fish. Using a steamer, steam for 8–10 minutes, or until fish is cooked. Remove the tray and place steamed ginger and garlic in the centre of the plate with steamed fish on top. Re-boil the broth and pour 60 ml (2 fl oz/¼ cup) over each fish. Garnish with finely sliced shiitake mushrooms, shredded carrot, spring onion and dill leaves and serve.

GINGER

Added to curries and stir-fries, ginger can be used to temper strong fish flavours and provide aroma to other dishes. Young ginger has thin skin and is more delicate than old ginger which has a much stronger flavour and a thick skin. It is said the calming effects of ginger help prevent morning sickness, aid digestion, relieve stomach-aches and reduce excess wind and mucus.

STIR-FRIED SCALLOPS WITH THAI HERBS

HOI SHELL PAD CHA

Serves 4

NUTRIENTS PER SERVING

Energy 164.79 kcal

Protein 19.4 g

Carbohydrate 18.68 g

Total fat 1.44 g

In a heavy wok, stir-fry chopped garlic over a low to medium heat, gradually adding half of the vegetable stock. Then add crushed bird's eye chillies and scallops. Stir-fry for 2–3 minutes until the scallops are half cooked, then add peppercorns and lesser galangal. Add more vegetable stock to moisten. Continue to cook for 1–2 minutes and season with oyster sauce, miso paste and honey. Sprinkle with sliced chillies and kaffir lime leaves. Remove from heat and serve with brown rice.

8 garlic cloves, chopped

400 ml (14 fl oz/1⅔ cups) vegetable stock (see Basics)

2 bird's eye chillies, crushed

400 g (14 oz) scallops

4 sprigs fresh peppercorns

30 g (1 oz) lesser galangal, peeled and julienned

4 tbsp oyster sauce

2 tbsp miso paste

2 tbsp honey

2 red and yellow chillies, seeded and finely sliced

4 kaffir lime leaves, torn

LESSER GALANGAL

Originally from China where it is used as a medicinal herb, lesser galangal is now widely grown in Indonesia and used as a spice. As with galangal, it has a calming and soothing affect on digestion. It is used against nausea, flatulence, indigestion, rheumatism, catarrh and enteritis. It also possesses tonic and antibacterial qualities. In India it is used as a body deodorizer and for bad breath. Both types of galangal have been used in Europe and Asia as an aphrodisiac for centuries.

STEAMED MUSSELS WITH SWEET BASIL

HOI MALAENG PHOO OB MOH DIN

Serves 4

NUTRIENTS PER SERVING

Energy 162.49 kcal

Protein 15.38 g

Carbohydrate 22.12 g

Total fat 2.62 g

40 ml (1½ fl oz/⅛ cup) vegetable stock (see Basics)
6 shallots, peeled and crushed
60 g (2¼ oz) galangal, peeled and thickly sliced
4 stalks lemongrass, diagonally sliced in 3 cm
(1¼ inch) lengths
10 kaffir lime leaves, torn
8 garlic cloves, crushed
1.2 kg (2 lb 10 oz) mussels, left whole and cleaned
4 handfuls Thai basil leaves
Serve with:
3 tbsp seafood dip (see Basics)

In a large saucepan, bring all ingredients, except basil and mussels to a boil, over a medium heat. Cover and simmer for 2–3 minutes. Add mussels; when cooked the shells will change colour and open. Sprinkle with Thai basil leaves. Place on a plate and serve with seafood dip.

CHEF'S TIP | Clean mussels with a brush under cold running water to remove sand and grit and debeard them by hand or with a pair of pliers. Debearding can kill the mussels so prepare them as close to cooking time as possible.

SCALLOP | Scallops provide a delicate flavour and a soft silky texture to any seafood dish. Although higher in saturated fats, they do provide valuable vitamins and minerals, including selenium, an antioxidant mineral that the body uses to remain calm, cobalt, a trace mineral, and vitamin B12.

STIR-FRIED SEAFOOD WITH CHILLI PASTE
PAD KHEE MAO TA LAY

Serves 4

NUTRIENTS PER SERVING
Energy 162.95 kcal
Protein 17.61 g
Carbohydrate 19.48 g
Total fat 1.9 g

In a heavy wok, stir-fry chopped garlic and chilli paste over a low to medium heat, gradually add a third of the vegetable stock. Then add king fish, prawns, scallops and squid and stir over a high heat. Add peppercorns and season with oyster sauce, miso paste, honey and unsweetened black soy sauce. Add remaining vegetable stock, sprinkle with sliced chillies and holy basil leaves and remove from heat. Serve with brown rice.

8 garlic cloves, chopped
1 tbsp fresh red chilli paste (see Basics)
250 ml (9 fl oz/1 cup) vegetable stock (see Basics)
120 g (4¼ oz) king fish, cubed
120 g (4¼ oz) prawns, peeled and de-veined
80 g (2⅔ oz) scallops
80 g (2⅔ oz) fresh squid cut into 1 cm (½ inch) wide rings
20 g (⅔ oz) green peppercorns
4 tbsp oyster sauce
3 tbsp miso paste
2 tbsp honey
2 tsp unsweetened black soy sauce
2 red and green bird's eye chillies, sliced
2 handfuls holy basil leaves

ROASTED CHICKEN WITH LEMONGRASS
GAI OB TA-KAI

Serves 4

NUTRIENTS PER SERVING
Energy 292.06 kcal
Protein 31.47 g
Carbohydrate 31.57 g
Total fat 4.91 g

140 ml (¼ pint/⅔ cup) vegetable stock (see Basics)
100 g (3½ oz) lemongrass, roughly chopped and crushed
4 tbsp honey
4 tbsp miso paste
4 tbsp soy sauce
1 tsp ground white pepper

MARINADE

In a saucepan, mix all ingredients together over a medium heat. Bring to a boil and simmer for 5 minutes, or until reduced by half. Drain, discard lemongrass and allow sauce to cool.

marinade
150 g (5½ oz) lemongrass, pressed and roughly chopped
480 g (1 lb 1 oz) chicken breast, skin removed
20 g (¾ oz) roasted sunflower seeds, to garnish
20 g (¾ oz) baked shredded lemongrass, finely diagonally sliced and baked at 180°C (360°F) for 10 minutes

ROASTED CHICKEN

Mix marinade and chopped lemongrass, add chicken and marinate for 30 minutes. Place chicken in a shallow baking tray and bake in the oven at 180°C (360°F) for 10 minutes. Remove the chicken from the baking tray, slice and place on a plate, pour sauce over, garnish with sunflower seeds and baked shredded lemongrass and serve. Note: if the sauce has become too thick add a little vegetable stock with the sauce in the baking tray and simmer before serving.

STIR-FRIED LAMB CHOPS WITH OYSTER SAUCE

NEUA KAE PAD NAM MON HOI

Serves 4

NUTRIENTS PER SERVING
Energy 235.75 kcal
Protein 22.84 g
Carbohydrate 22.19 g
Total fat 22.19 g

8 garlic cloves, chopped
400 ml (14 fl oz/1⅔ cups) vegetable stock (see Basics)
4 tbsp miso paste
4 tbsp oyster sauce
2 tbsp honey
1 tbsp unsweetened black soy sauce
400 g (14 oz) lamb chops, trimmed of fat and cut into bite-size pieces
240 g (9 oz) bok choy, leaves trimmed
200 g (7 oz) straw mushrooms, boiled for 2 minutes and drained
3 spring onions, cut into 5 cm (2 inch) lengths
1 red chilli, seeded and finely sliced
pinch of ground white pepper

In a heavy wok, stir-fry garlic using vegetable stock. Once fragrant, add miso paste, oyster sauce, honey and unsweetened black soy sauce. Add lamb and stir-fry for 3–4 minutes, or until half cooked, and add bok choy leaves and cooked straw mushrooms. Once bok choy is soft and lamb is well cooked, sprinkle with spring onions, red chilli and ground white pepper. Remove from heat and serve with brown rice.

STIR-FRIED BEEF WITH CHILLI AND HOLY BASIL
PAD KRA PRAO NEUA

Serves 4

NUTRIENTS PER SERVING
Energy 197.08 kcal
Protein 22.37 g
Carbohydrate 9.92 g
Total fat 7.23 g

5 bird's eye chillies, chopped
8 garlic cloves, chopped
1½ tbsp vegetable stock (see Basics)
400 g (14 oz) beef tenderloin, trimmed
and sliced into bite-size pieces
3 tbsp soy sauce
1 tbsp honey
1 tsp sliced red chilli
2 handfuls holy basil leaves

In a heavy wok, stir-fry bird's eye chillies and garlic using half of the vegetable stock. Once fragrant, add sliced beef tenderloin and cook for several minutes. Moisten with remaining vegetable stock and season with soy sauce and honey. Add sliced chilli and holy basil leaves and remove from heat. Serve with brown rice.

HOLY BASIL

Known as holy basil because it is planted around temples, the leaves are smaller and a distinctive reddish-purple in colour. It has a strong odour and is traditionally used fresh in strong flavoured dishes such as fish curries or chilli-flavoured stir-fries. The leaves aid digestion and the strong scent is said to repel mosquitoes.

STIR-FRIED MUSHROOMS WITH FRESH GINGER
HED PAD KING

Serves 4

80 g (2²/₃ oz) onions, sliced
6 garlic cloves, chopped
140 ml (¼ pint/²/₃ cup) vegetable stock (see Basics)
200 g (7 oz) wood ear mushrooms, trimmed and
cut into bite-size pieces
100 g (3½ oz) dried white wood ear mushrooms,
soaked in warm water for 10 minutes
100 g (3½ oz) oyster mushrooms
100 g (3½ oz) red pepper, diagonally sliced
80 g (2²/₃ oz) carrots, julienned
30 g (1 oz) spring onions, cut into 4 cm
(1½ inch) lengths
30 g (1 oz) ginger, julienned
3 tbsp soy sauce
½ tbsp honey
5 g (⅛ oz) dried ginger, sliced

NUTRIENTS PER SERVING

Energy 99.32 kcal
Protein 3.07 g
Carbohydrate 21.73 g
Total fat 0.47 g

Heat a wok or heavy-based frying pan. Once very hot, stir-fry onions and garlic using half of the vegetable stock. Add mushrooms, red pepper, carrot, spring onion and ginger and cook for 3 minutes. Add remaining stock, soy sauce and honey. Bring to a boil and remove from heat, garnish with dried ginger slices. Be careful not to overcook this dish; the vegetables, while cooked, should remain crunchy.

Wood ear mushrooms look like ears growing out of trees, hence the name. A brownish-black colour, this mushroom has a thick, firm skin with a slightly crunchy texture and earthy flavour. Commonly served in spicy soups and, as with most edible fungi, it has immune boosting properties.

WOOD EAR MUSHROOM

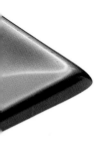

STIR-FRIED TOFU WITH HOLY BASIL
PAD KRA PRAO TAO HOO

Serves 4

NUTRIENTS PER SERVING
Energy 114.35 kcal
Protein 8.81 g
Carbohydrate 13.67 g
Total fat 2.94 g

5 bird's eye chillies, chopped
8 garlic cloves, chopped
100 ml (3½ fl oz/½ cup) vegetable stock (see Basics)
280 g (10 oz) hard tofu, cubed
80 g (2⅔ oz) string beans, cut diagonally
in 5 cm (2 inch) lengths
160 g (5¾ oz) straw mushrooms, halved
120 g (4¼ oz) baby corn, cut diagonally
in 5 cm (2 inch) lengths
2½ tbsp soy sauce
2 tbsp oyster sauce
1½ tbsp honey
3 red and green chillies, seeded and finely sliced
4 handfuls holy basil leaves

In a heavy wok, stir-fry bird's eye chillies and garlic using just half of the vegetable stock. Once fragrant, add tofu, string beans, straw mushrooms and baby corn and cook for several minutes. Moisten with remaining vegetable stock and season with soy sauce, oyster sauce and honey. Add sliced chillies and holy basil. Remove from heat and serve with brown rice.

CHILLIES

Chillies have positive effects on blood pressure, clotting and circulation as well as on the metabolism. Rich in vitamin C, red chillies are a useful circulatory stimulant that can reduce the risk of cardiovascular disease. The larger the chilli the milder the flavour. Bird's eye chillies are very small and therefore very hot. If used in moderation, all chillies are a great tonic for the body.

PUMPKIN

Pumpkin is a member of the gourd family. Its flesh is fibrous and firm, and has an earthy, sometimes sweet, taste. It is used in Asian cooking in a number of ways, both savoury and sweet. When buying pumpkin check that the skin is not pitted and that the stem is still intact. Rich in beta-carotene, pumpkins can help protect the body against heart disease.

STIR-FRIED PUMPKIN WITH CHILLI AND BASIL
FAKTHONG PAD BAI HORAPA

Serves 4

NUTRIENTS PER SERVING
Energy 149.35 kcal
Protein 3.35 g
Carbohydrate 34.25 g
Total fat 0.36 g

8 garlic cloves, chopped
120 g (4¼ oz) onions, halved and sliced into strips
100 ml (3½ fl oz/⅜ cup) vegetable stock (see Basics)
600 g (1 lb 5 oz) pumpkin, peeled and cubed
2½ tbsp soy sauce
2 tbsp oyster sauce
1½ tbsp honey
4 handfuls Thai basil leaves, to garnish
3 red chillies, seeded and finely sliced, to garnish

In a heavy wok, stir-fry garlic and onion using half of the vegetable stock, until browned. Add pumpkin cubes, moisten with remaining vegetable stock and stir constantly until pumpkin is cooked. Season with soy sauce, oyster sauce and honey. Sprinkle with Thai basil leaves and sliced red chilli. Serve with brown rice.

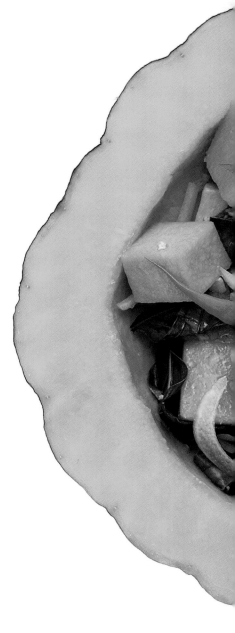

RICE/
NOODLES

Rice and noodles are a staple in Asian diets and many dishes including appetizers, mains and desserts feature them. Although white rice and noodles are the norm, much greater nutrition and fibre are provided in wholegrain varieties. Indeed, normal brown rice, red and black rice, and wild rice will boost nutritional values up to six times more than that given by refined rice. Even brown rice noodles and wholewheat noodles will ensure much higher levels of nutrition.

Beat 6 egg whites until fluffy then pour into a
heat-proof container and steam for 10–15 minutes.
The egg white will become firm and easy to cut.
Remove from the steam and cut into cubes.

STEAMED EGG WHITE

STIR-FRIED RICE NOODLES
PAAD THAI

Serves 4

NUTRIENTS PER SERVING
Energy 316.48 kcal
Protein 19.88 g
Carbohydrate 45.97 g
Total fat 7.7 g

150 g (5½ oz) honey
125 ml (4 fl oz/½ cup) tamarind juice (see Basics)
250 ml (9 fl oz/1 cup) water
6 shallots, finely sliced
5 tbsp soy sauce

8 shallots, sliced
5 tbsp vegetable stock (see Basics)
60 g (2¼ oz) preserved turnip, chopped
120 g (4¼ oz) hard tofu, diced and
pan-roasted until golden brown
120 g (4¼ oz) steamed egg white cubes (see opposite)
200 g (7 oz) soaked brown rice noodles
180 g (6 oz) prawns, peeled, de-veined and
poached quickly in boiling water
320 ml (11½ fl oz/1¼ cup) paad Thai sauce
120 g (4¼ oz) bean sprouts
40 g (1½ oz) garlic chives, cut into 3 cm (1 inch) lengths
8 tbsp ground roasted almonds
Serve with:
20 g (¾ oz) bean sprouts
½ sliced shallot
2 tbsp garlic chives, chopped
1 tbsp ground roasted almonds
1 tsp dried chilli powder
1 lime wedge

PAAD THAI SAUCE

In a saucepan, combine all ingredients and bring to a boil. Simmer for 20–25 minutes or until the sauce has reduced by a third. Any leftover sauce can be refrigerated.

STIR-FRIED RICE NOODLES

In a wok or large heavy-based pan, stir-fry shallots in 4 tbsp vegetable stock. Stir-fry for 15 seconds then add preserved turnip, tofu and steamed egg white cubes. Toss to cook quickly. Add noodles, prawns and paad Thai sauce. Toss well. Add bean sprouts, garlic chives and ground almonds. Cook for 2–3 minutes, stirring carefully. If the noodles become too dry add more stock. Serve with bean sprouts, shallot, garlic chives, ground almonds, dried chilli powder and lime wedge.

BEEF AND LEMONGRASS NOODLE SOUP
KUAY TIEW NEUA

Serves 4

NUTRIENTS PER SERVING

Energy 237.18 kcal

Protein 18 g

Carbohydrate 32.94 g

Total fat 4.18 g

300 g (10½ oz) lean minced beef

300 g (10½ oz) carrots, peeled and finely chopped

200 g (7 oz) lemongrass, finely chopped

200 g (7 oz) onions, finely chopped

60 g (2¼ oz) celery, chopped

30 g (1 oz) coriander roots, finely chopped

1 egg

2 L (3½ pints/2 quarts) cold water

3 pieces star anise

2 cinnamon sticks

1 tbsp black peppercorns

12 garlic cloves, halved and seared on cut-side for 3–4 minutes

120 g (4¼ oz) pineapple, peeled and cut into chunks

90 ml (3¼ fl oz/½ cup) soy sauce

800 ml (1½ pints/3⅓ cups) beef and lemongrass stock

320 g (11½ oz) soaked brown rice noodles

200 g (7 oz) bean sprouts, soaked in tepid water for 15–20 minutes

160 g (5½ oz) bok choy, sliced into bite-size pieces

180 g (6 oz) cooked beef fillets, sliced into 4 pieces

tip of Chinese celery leaves to garnish

tip of Thai basil to garnish

BEEF AND LEMONGRASS STOCK

Makes 2 litres (3½ pints/2 quarts). In a large mixing bowl, combine minced beef and chopped carrots, lemongrass, onions, celery, coriander roots and egg. Transfer mixture to a large saucepan. Add cold water and place over a high heat. Stir constantly and bring to a rolling boil. Reduce to a simmer and stop stirring. Add star anise, cinnamon sticks, black peppercorns, seared garlic, pineapple and soy sauce. Simmer for 2 hours. Remove from heat, cool and sieve mixture, keeping the stock. Leftover stock can be kept in the freezer.

NOODLES

In a saucepan, bring the beef and lemongrass stock to a boil. In another pan, plunge brown rice noodles, bean sprouts and bok choy in 2 L (3½ pints/8½ cups) of boiling water for about 30 seconds, then drain. The noodles should be al dente. Place the noodles in a serving bowl and arrange bean sprouts, bok choy and cooked beef fillet on top. Pour the beef and lemongrass stock over, garnish with Chinese celery and Thai basil and serve immediately.

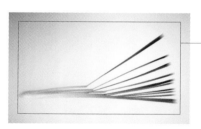

LEMONGRASS

One of the most popular herbs of South-East Asia, lemongrass is a vital flavour in Thai curry pastes. Its medicinal properties are well known in Asian, Chinese and Western herbal medicine and, when taken internally, its antiseptic properties are useful for the treatment of stomach-aches, fevers, flu, to treat coughs and clean wounds. It can also be used to stimulate circulation, relieve headaches and as a diuretic.

CHICKEN CURRY NOODLE SOUP

KHAO SOI GAI

Serves 4

CHINESE KALE

Chinese kale, also known as Chinese broccoli or gai lan, is a leafy vegetable eaten widely throughout Asia. When young and tender it can be cooked whole, the same way as broccoli. Slightly older shoots have more flavour but the stems may need peeling and chopping.

550 ml (19 fl oz/2¼ cups) vegetable stock (see Basics)
100 ml (3½ fl oz/½ cup) coconut milk
10 medium shallots, finely sliced
3 tbsp miso paste
2½ tbsp honey
1 tbsp roasted chilli paste (see Basics)
2 tsp curry powder
160 g (5¾ oz) chicken breast, sliced into bite-size pieces

CHICKEN CURRY SOUP

In a saucepan, combine all ingredients, except chicken, and bring to a boil. Simmer for 8–10 minutes. Then bring back to the boil and add sliced chicken, stir and cook for 4–5 minutes.

180 g (6 oz) brown rice noodles, soaked in tepid water for 15–20 minutes
160 g (5½ oz) Chinese kale, sliced
100 g (3½ oz) baby corn
100 g (3½ oz) carrots, peeled and diced
Serve with:
2 sliced roasted shallots
2 sliced fresh shallots
1 tbsp roasted chilli paste (see Basics)
1 tbsp chopped coriander
1 tbsp soy sauce
lime wedges

NOODLES

In a saucepan, bring 2 L (3½ pints/8½ cups) water to a boil and plunge the noodles, Chinese kale, baby corn and carrot for about 30 seconds then drain. The noodles should be al dente. Place the noodles, Chinese kale, baby corn and carrot into a serving bowl. Pour over the chicken curry soup and serve immediately with sliced roasted shallots, sliced fresh shallots, roasted chilli paste, coriander, soy sauce and lime wedges on the side.

THAI RICE CURRY WITH HERBED CHICKEN
KHAO MOK GAI

Serves 4

NUTRIENTS PER SERVING
Energy 403.5 kcal
Protein 27.46 g
Carbohydrate 56.84 g
Total fat 6.92 g

Cinnamon sticks are made from long pieces of bark from various laurel trees that are rolled, pressed and dried. The type of cinnamon used in Thailand is from the Cassia tree. Cinnamon has a sweet, woody fragrance in both ground and stick forms. Rich in therapeutic essential oils, cinnamon warms the body and enhances digestion. It boosts metabolism and is thus useful for weight loss. It is also good for diabetics as it stimulates insulin production.

CINNAMON

300 ml (10 fl oz/1¼ cup) rice vinegar
260 g (9 oz) honey
360 g (12 oz) cucumber, peeled, cored and finely chopped
4 tbsp finely chopped long red chillies
3 tbsp chopped coriander

CUCUMBER RELISH

In a saucepan, bring vinegar and honey to a boil. Stir frequently until the honey has dissolved and continue to cook for 10–15 minutes. Remove from heat. Once cooled, add cucumber, chillies and coriander and stir well. Set aside until ready to serve.

60 ml (2¼ fl oz/¼ cup) coconut milk
1 shallot, finely chopped
2 garlic cloves, finely chopped
1 tbsp finely chopped fresh ginger
4 chicken breasts, skinned and boned
1 tbsp curry powder
¼ tsp turmeric powder
300 g (10½ oz) brown jasmine rice
3 tbsp soy sauce
1 tbsp miso paste
4 cardamom pods
1 bay leaf
1 cinnamon stick

THAI RICE CURRY WITH HERBED CHICKEN

Heat the coconut milk in a large saucepan or casserole dish which has a lid. Add shallot, garlic and ginger, and cook over a low to medium heat for 3–5 minutes. Add chicken and turn up the heat until it is evenly browned. Add curry powder and turmeric powder and stir well to evenly coat chicken. Add rice, soy sauce and miso paste, and stir well. Pour in 250 ml (9 fl oz/1 cup) water and stir well. Add cardamom pods, bay leaf and cinnamon stick. Cover and bring to a boil. Reduce heat and simmer gently for 30–35 minutes or until the rice is cooked and tender. Remove from heat and leave for 10 minutes leaving the lid on. After 10 minutes, fluff the rice with a fork and discard cardamom pods, bay leaf and cinnamon stick. Serve rice curry warm with cucumber relish on the side.

RICE SOUP WITH SLICED FISH
KHAO TOM PLA

Serves 4

NUTRIENTS PER SERVING
Energy 153.59 kcal
Protein 19.46 g
Carbohydrate 14.22 g
Total fat 2.32 g

50 g (1¾ oz) wild rice
100 g (3½ oz) brown rice
800 ml (1½ pints/3⅓ cups) vegetable stock (see Basics)
320 g (11½ oz) red snapper fillet, sliced diagonally into bite-size pieces
4 tbsp soy sauce
pinch of ground black pepper
15 g (½ oz) fresh ginger, finely sliced
15 g (½ oz) chopped Chinese celery
15 g (½ oz) chopped spring onion

In a saucepan, bring 1.3 L (2¼ pints/1⅓ quarts) water to a boil, add wild rice and stir constantly over a medium heat for 40 minutes. Add brown rice to the pan and cook for a further 30 minutes. The rice will expand. Once rice is cooked, add vegetable stock and bring back to a boil. Add sliced red snapper fillet. Season with soy sauce and ground black pepper. Sprinkle with ginger, Chinese celery, spring onion and serve.

WILD RICE

Wild rice is hardly related to rice; it is actually an aquatic cereal and from a different botanical family. Compared to white rice, it is nutritionally superior and contains twice as much protein, six times as much thiamine (vitamin B1), niacin (vitamin B3) and iron, and 20 times as much riboflavin (vitamin B2). Wild rice is also a good source of potassium, phosphorus, and the amino acid, lysine. The whole grain fibre content makes wild rice a good source of sustained energy.

DESSERTS

Thai desserts naturally lend themselves to spa cuisine with the absence of wheat, dairy and gluten. Young coconut with its ambrosial scent and emollient qualities, fresh mango with its antioxidant properties, lime adding a dose of vitamin C and rice, tapioca and taro forming the basis of many desserts, all provide a welcome change for those with food intolerances.

WATER CHESTNUT WITH COCONUT CUSTARD

TAGO BAI TOEY

Makes 12 pieces

NUTRIENTS PER PIECE

Energy 50.13 kcal

Protein 0.87 g

Carbohydrate 5.54 g

Total fat 3.03 g

WATER CHESTNUT

Dissolve honey and mung bean flour in pandan water and add water chestnuts. Transfer to a heavy-based wok on a medium-low heat and stir constantly. Once thickened, spoon the mixture into the prepared pandan packets.

2 tbsp honey

15 g (½ oz) mung bean flour

4 pandan leaves, puréed in 250 ml (9 fl oz/ 1 cup) water to make pandan juice

50 g (1¾ oz) water chestnuts, cut into small cubes

12 pandan leaves, prepared into square packets (see below)

COCONUT CUSTARD

Mix coconut milk and rice flour together, place in a small pan and bring to a boil. Stir frequently until the mixture thickens. Quickly spoon some mixture on top of the prepared water chestnut. Leave to cool before serving in the packets.

150 ml (¼ pint/⅔ cup) coconut milk

15 g (½ oz) rice flour

PANDAN PACKETS

To make packets, cut pandan leaf to 15 cm (6 inch) long and 3.5 cm (1½ inch) wide (fig. 1). Using a spatula fold the leaf every 3 cm (1 inch) making 5 sections (fig. 2). To make the base, fold the leaf lengthways 1.5 cm (¾ inch) deep. Snip along the 1.5 cm (¾ inch) deep folds and fold each section, inserting each flap so they overlap with each other to form the base (fig. 3). The last flap should insert inside the base so that the packet holds firm (fig. 4).

CHEF'S TIP Spoon the water chestnut mixture into each pandan packet so they are all half full. Once cooled, spoon the coconut custard to fill each packet. Allow to cool and serve. If pandan leaves are not available replace with espresso, or small porcelain, cups.

STEAMED THAI BANANA WITH GRATED COCONUT

KHA NOM KLUAY

Makes 12 pieces

NUTRIENTS PER PIECE

Energy 107.82 kcal

Protein 0.95 g

Carbohydrate 18.66 g

Total fat 3.51 g

6 Thai bananas, peeled and mashed
100 g (3½ oz) brown sugar
90 g (3¼ oz) grated coconut
50 g (1¾ oz) rice flour
50 ml (2 fl oz/¼ cup) coconut milk
12 g (½ oz) tapioca flour

Beat all ingredients with just half of the grated coconut, until evenly blended. Place in small porcelain cups and smoothen the surface. Sprinkle over remaining coconut and steam for 30–35 minutes. Leave to cool and serve.

Bananas are rich in carbohydrates, fibre, potassium and folic acid. Unripe bananas contain mostly starches. However, as they ripen, these starches are converted to fructose, making bananas a high energy food. 100 g (3½ oz) banana provides 12% RDA of potassium, 12% RDA of fibre and substantial doses of the antioxidants beta-carotene and vitamin C. Potassium lowers blood pressure and folic acid is beneficial for those preparing for pregnancy. Bananas can be used for the relief of both constipation and diarrhoea.

BANANA

STEAMED TAPIOCA WITH GRATED COCONUT

KHA NOM MAN

Makes 12 pieces

NUTRIENTS PER PIECE
Energy 89.47 kcal
Protein 0.72 g
Carbohydrate 15.91 g
Total fat 2.86 g

250 g (9 oz) tapioca root, peeled,
sliced and roughly chopped
200 ml (7 fl oz/1 cup) water
80 g (2⅔ oz) honey
10 g (¼ oz) mung bean flour
10 g (¼ oz) rice flour
100 g (3½ oz) grated coconut,
steamed for 6 minutes

Blend chopped tapioca root with water, honey, mung bean flour and rice flour. Spread on a rimmed plate and smoothen the surface. Steam for 35–40 minutes, allow to cool and then cut into 2.5 cm (1 inch) cubes. Coat with steamed grated coconut.

GLAZED WATER CHESTNUT IN COCONUT SYRUP

TAB TIM KROB

Serves 4

NUTRIENTS PER SERVING
Energy 228.56 kcal
Protein 1.81 g
Carbohydrate 34.88 g
Total fat 10.73 g

160 g (5½ oz) water chestnuts, cut into small cubes
40 g (1½ oz) grenadine
40 g (1½ oz) tapioca flour
200 ml (7 fl oz/1 cup) coconut milk
80 g (2⅔ oz) honey
20 g (¾ oz) grated young coconut flesh
20 g (¾ oz) sliced jackfruit
200 g (7 oz) crushed ice

To prepare glazed water chestnuts, soak water chestnut cubes in grenadine for 20–30 minutes and blend with tapioca flour. Discard any excess flour and place in a pan of boiling water for 1–2 minutes until cooked. The cubes will become glazed and float. Remove from heat and transfer to cold water. Replace the cold water 2–3 times to ensure they are fully cooled. To prepare coconut syrup, mix coconut milk with honey and set aside. Place glazed water chestnuts, coconut syrup, young coconut flesh and jackfruit in a bowl, top with crushed ice and serve.

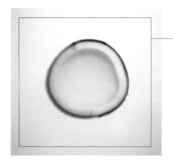

COCONUT

All parts of the coconut are used in Thai cuisine, from the juice to the flesh and even the shell for cooking utensils and pots. Coconut milk is a hallmark of Thai cooking and young coconut water is nature's very own isotonic drink. A good source of potassium, vitamin C, calcium and magnesium, it balances the blood and the fatty acids are burned for energy rather than stored as fat, hence raising metabolism and aiding weight loss.

TARO CAKE
KHA NOM MOH GAENG

Serves 8

NUTRIENTS PER SERVING

Energy 428.32 kcal

Protein 8.88 g

Carbohydrate 53.07 g

Total fat 19.81 g

500 ml (18 fl oz/2¼ cups) coconut milk
350 g (12 oz) grated palm sugar
150 g (5½ oz) taro, peeled, cubed
and steamed for 15–20 minutes
35 g (1¼ oz) rice flour
10 egg whites
3 whole eggs

Mix all ingredients by hand using a shredded banana or pandan leaf. Strain, and pour the mixture into a square baking dish, or into separate ramekin dishes. Place on a deep baking tray in 2.5 cm (1 inch) water. Place the bain-marie in the oven and bake at 145°C (300°F) for 20 minutes or until the cake is cooked. Leave to cool and cut cake as desired.

CHEF'S TIP | Mixing the ingredients by hand will reduce any air bubbles and ensure the palm sugar is fully dissolved. Using a pandan leaf will release a pleasant flavour into the mixture.

BLACK STICKY RICE WITH MANGO
KHAO NIEW MA MUANG

Makes 15 pieces

NUTRIENTS PER PIECE
Energy 259.15 kcal
Protein 4.15 g
Carbohydrate 51.21 g
Total fat 4.59 g

300 g (10½ oz) black glutinous rice
300 g (10½ oz) white glutinous rice
180 g (6 oz) brown sugar
225 ml (8 fl oz/1 cup) coconut milk
750 g (1 lb 10 oz) ripe mangoes,
peeled and cut into bite-size wedges

Soak black glutinous rice and white glutinous rice separately in water overnight. Drain and combine. In a steamer, steam rice for 30–40 minutes. In a saucepan, over a medium heat, combine brown sugar and coconut milk and simmer for 7–10 minutes, stir constantly and ensure sugar has dissolved. Pour milk mixture into a large mixing bowl, add cooked sticky rice and combine. Cover the mixing bowl with a lid or cling film and allow rice to absorb liquid for 30 minutes. Form the sticky rice into oval shapes by hand; there should be enough for 15 pieces. Place mango wedges on top and serve.

In the West, mango is only eaten when ripe. In Asia, unripe green mango is also eaten regularly. Ripe mango provides anti-oxidant carotenoids (which are converted by the body to vitamin A), and is considered an anti-depressant. In the green form, it makes a popular snack (Thais often dip it in a mix of chilli and sugar) and it can be used as an addition to spicy salads or soups. It's commonly used as a remedy for nausea due to the sour taste.

MANGO

APPENDICES

Basics / Glossary / Index / Acknowledgements

BASICS

2 cm (1 inch) piece galangal, peeled and finely sliced
3 cm (1½ inch) finely sliced lemongrass
3 coriander roots, finely chopped
10 green bird's eye chillies
1 tsp coriander seeds
1 tsp finely chopped kaffir lime peel
1 medium shallot, sliced
3 garlic cloves
1 tsp toasted shrimp paste, toasted in banana leaf for 4–5 minutes

GREEN CURRY PASTE

Using a pestle and mortar, pound galangal, lemongrass, coriander roots, chillies, coriander seeds, kaffir lime peel, shallot, garlic and shrimp paste until smooth. Ingredients should be added in that order. Before adding each ingredient ensure that the previous has been mashed until smooth. Using a blender, add little by little of the hard ingredients. Soften with a little water or soy sauce. Pulp until puréed.

2 cm (1 inch) piece galangal, peeled and chopped
3 cm (1½ inch) lemongrass, chopped
6 large dried red chillies, seeded and soaked in water until soft
1 tsp chopped kaffir lime peel
3 coriander roots, chopped
1 tsp coriander seeds
½ tsp cumin seeds
1 medium shallot
3 garlic cloves
1½ tsp toasted shrimp paste: toasted in a banana leaf for 4–5 minutes

RED CURRY PASTE

Using a pestle and mortar, pound galangal, lemongrass, dried red chillies, kaffir lime peel, coriander roots, coriander and cumin seeds, shallot, garlic and shrimp paste until smooth. Ingredients should be added in that order. Before adding each ingredient ensure that the previous has been mashed until smooth. Using a blender, add little by little of the hard ingredients. Soften with a little water or soy sauce. Pulp until puréed.

6 dried red chillies, seeded and roasted
3 cm (1½ inch) piece lemongrass, chopped and roasted
2 cm (1 inch) piece galangal, peeled, sliced and roasted
1 tsp roasted and finely chopped kaffir lime peel
8 tbsp ground almonds
3 garlic cloves, peeled and roasted
1½ medium shallots, chopped and roasted
2 cloves, roasted and ground
1 tsp nutmeg
1 tsp ground mace
2 tsp ground cumin seeds
2 tsp ground coriander seeds
1 tsp ground cinnamon
1 tbsp soy sauce

MASSAMAN CURRY PASTE

Using a pestle and mortar, pound dried red chilli, lemongrass, galangal, kaffir lime peel,, ground almonds, garlic, shallots, cloves, nutmeg, mace, cumin seeds, coriander seeds and cinnamon until smooth. Ingredients should be added in that order. Gradually pour in soy sauce to moisten. Ensure each ingredient is smooth before adding the next.

FRESH CHILLI PASTE

2 medium shallots
2 cloves garlic
3 coriander roots, roughly chopped
1 red chilli, roughly chopped

Pound all ingredients with a pestle and mortar or blend in a food processor.

ROASTED CHILLI PASTE

10 medium shallots, peeled, skewered and roasted until soft
15 garlic cloves, peeled, skewered and roasted until soft
20 large dried red chillies, seeds discarded and roasted until crispy
3 1/3 tbsp palm sugar
2 tbsp miso paste
2 tbsp soy sauce
1 1/2 tbsp tamarind juice

In a food processor, blend shallots, garlic and chillies together. In a pan, stir-fry over a low heat, add palm sugar, miso paste, soy sauce and tamarind juice. Stir constantly and simmer until thickened.

FRESH SEAFOOD DIP

100 ml (3 1/2 fl oz/ 1/2 cup) lime juice
100 ml (3 1/2 fl oz/ 1/2 cup) soy sauce
4 tbsp honey
15 bird's eye chillies
3 garlic cloves
7 coriander stems with roots, chopped

Blend all ingredients in a food processor until smooth.

TAMARIND JUICE

150 g (5 1/2 oz) dried tamarind
600 ml (20 fl oz/2 1/2 cups) warm water

In a bowl, combine dried tamarind and warm water then squeeze or press the mixture until the tamarind pulp is released and only the fibrous strands remain.

VEGETABLE STOCK

Makes 1 litre (1 3/4 pints/4 1/4 cups)
2 red tomatoes
1/2 small cabbage (preferably Chinese cabbage)
1/2 brown onion
2 pieces Chinese celery or 1 stalk of celery
1 medium carrot
3 coriander roots
1.5 L (2 3/4 pints/6 1/3 cups) water

In a large saucepan, combine all ingredients and bring to a boil. Simmer for 1 hour. Strain and discard the vegetables. The vegetable stock is best fresh but it can be refrigerated for 2–3 days, or even frozen. It is prone to absorbing other flavours in the refrigerator so ensure the container is airtight.

GLOSSARY

BROWN RICE NOODLES

With all the health benefits of brown rice, these noodles offer a healthy alternative to regular refined white rice noodles. White rice has half the amount of zinc than the brown variety, and even less magnesium and chromium—not to mention the loss of vitamins and fibre. Brown rice noodles are also a great substitute for wheat-based pastas. With some creativity they can be used in a variety of ways, from traditional Thai cuisine to Italian dishes.

CHINESE DATES

Also named jujube or red date, Chinese dates are olive-shaped and have a thin dark red skin and a mucilaginous, sweet white flesh. Medicinally, Chinese dates are high in vitamin C, they can be used to calm nerves, improve blood quality and are believed to cure insomnia.

CRAB

Known for its tender, sweet flesh, crab has long been a favourite seafood. Although higher in cholesterol (100 g (3½ oz) gives 33 per cent of your recommended daily amount), it is still low in fat and has a good ratio of polyunsaturated fats. Crabmeat is also nutritionally high in immune-building zinc and protein, calcium, and iron.

GALANGAL

Galangal, an aromatic rhizome also known as Chinese ginger, is well used in Thai cuisine. Although it resembles ginger, its aroma is closer to that of citrus fruit. It has a calming effect on the stomach and is traditionally used for indigestion, nausea, seasickness and excess gas. A warming herb, galangal is used to balance out an excess of fluid in the body and improve sluggish metabolism or digestion. The digestive impact of galangal is further increased if an infusion is made by steeping a piece in hot water. Galangal contains potassium, calcium, iron, vitamin B3 and phosphorus.

GARLIC

Garlic is seen as nature's antibiotic and has been used medicinally since biblical times. The main antibiotic properties come from the active constituent allicin, the pungent oily liquid. Garlic also contains a high sulphur content—a warming element that helps to purify the body. It has anti-viral properties, helps lower both blood pressure and cholesterol, it promotes healthy intestines, and is beneficial for respiratory ailments. Garlic is best eaten raw as cooking removes some flavour and aroma and also breaks down the medicinal constituents. Consuming fresh parsley after eating garlic can help to freshen the breath and neutralize the garlic odour.

GLASS NOODLES

Also referred to as cellophane noodles in Vietnam and spring rain noodles in Japan, glass noodles are an important ingredient in Thai cuisine. They are fine, dry and transparent and made from green mung bean starch. Glass noodles begin completely flavourless and actually take on the taste of the sauce or broth that accompanies them. They may be soaked for about 5–7 minutes in warm water before boiling, which will also help when cutting into shorter lengths.

MIANG KHAM LEAF

Miang means wrap in Thai and the leaf is so named because it is used to wrap ingredients, making a healthy Thai snack or entrée. The miang kham (betel) leaf has a unique aroma and a slightly bitter flavour. With fresh lime juice squeezed over, it makes an ideal appetizer—the bitter taste of the two combined will stimulate the digestive secretions. Miang kham may be difficult to find in some western countries so any herbaceous leaf, for example lettuce, can be used instead.

MISO PASTE

Miso—also known as bean paste—is made from cooked, mashed, salted and fermented soy beans. It varies in colour, texture and saltiness and is used to flavour soups, salad dressings, sauces, curries and marinades. The lighter pastes have been more quickly fermented and are therefore milder in flavour. The darker are stronger and more mature. Miso paste is available both sweet and salty, but the dark varieties are always salty. It's widely used in Japan, miso soup being the most common usage, and is used in Thai spa cuisine to add saltiness.

MUNG BEAN FLOUR

Mung beans contain between 19–25 per cent protein, 60 per cent carbohydrate and 4 per cent fibre. They are rich in the amino acid lysine and provide potassium, calcium, magnesium and iron as well as thiamine, riboflavin and niacin. The starch, or flour, is commonly used to make vermicelli and sheets for making savoury rolls, as well as in Asian desserts.

PALM SUGAR

This comes from the sap of the flower head of palms. When boiled, the sap produces a heavy and moist sugar. It varies in colour, from honey to dark brown, and in consistency. Usually bought in solid form, it should be grated for easy measuring.

PANDAN LEAF

The pandan (screwpine) leaf is used in a similar way to vanilla. Unique in flavour, foods cooked with, and in, pandan leaves easily take on the subtle flavours. Strips of pandan leaves are commonly used to make decorative woven baskets, from which rice, desserts or other food items can be served. It's believed that pandan can help maintain a healthy heart and liver, relieve fevers and soothe sore throats.

POMELO

Extremely popular in South-East Asia, the pomelo is the largest citrus fruit. Protected by a thick white membrane, the large juice sacs can be broken up and used in salads or eaten as a snack. When buying, pick one that feels heavier than it looks.

POMFRET

With its firm white flesh and delicate flavour, pomfret is one of the most popular varieties of fish used in cuisines across Asia and is suitable for all methods of cooking. The cooked flesh of the fish will maintain its moisture and the meat will fall away from the bones with ease. White fish, such as pomfret and garoupa, provides a good source of iodine, and is one of the best sources of protein due to its low saturated fat content.

RICE FLOUR

Rice flour is used as the base for all kinds of noodles, pastries and sweets. It acts as a binder, and as a coating to add crunchiness. It is sold in packets and is a pale creamy colour.

SHRIMP PASTE

This is a very strong-smelling paste made from fermented prawns. Shrimp paste is sold throughout Asia and is available in many different forms. Some are firm cakes and must be cut into blocks or slices. Some are a thick paste that can be spooned. All varieties are used for flavouring and to add protein. If it is being served with uncooked ingredients, it must be roasted first. Do this under the grill for 2–3 minutes each side, wrapped in banana leaf (or aluminium foil) so that the smell does not permeate the house.

STAR ANISE

Star anise is an attractive star shaped spice, and is an important constituent of Chinese Five Spice Powder. The liquorice-flavoured spice can be chewed after meals to calm the stomach and aid digestion, and has traditionally been used to relieve colic and rheumatism.

TAPIOCA

Tapioca (cassava) is a refined starch derived from the peeled and grated tapioca root. The juice is extracted and the pulp is soaked in water then kneaded to release the starch grains. Fibres are strained and the residue is heated until it forms balls, or pearls, of tapioca. The flour is commonly used in Thai cuisine, its large grains absorbing water more quickly and at lower temperatures than wheat or rice flour. Commonly in Thailand, the translucent balls of cooked tapioca are floated in drinks and liquid desserts.

THAI AUBERGINE

The aubergine is an essential ingredient in curry dishes. The smaller Thai versions are generally white or green and are round and golf ball-sized. In curries, Thai aubergines should be quartered and cooked in the curry sauce so that they can absorb the flavour and become softer. They can be substituted by the larger purple aubergines if the Thai variety cannot be found. Pea aubergines grow in clusters, they are very small in size and slightly bitter in flavour. These should be cooked whole.

THAI BASIL

Basil has aromatic qualities reminiscent of anise or liquorice when cooked, and is therapeutic not only for the senses but for the digestion too. Thai basil (also known as sweet basil) contains a high level of the antioxidant beta-carotene, as well as the minerals calcium, potassium, magnesium and iron. It has antibacterial, carminative and antispasmodic properties and is traditionally used for digestive disturbances and bacterial infections. Thai basil can also improve the blood circulation around the body, and has been used for relief of headaches, or for improving attention and focus.

INDEX

ACKNOWLEDGEMENTS

The publishers would like to thank the following for their contribution to the book:

Joy Menzies
Paul Linder
Jeff Nieuwenhuizen
Sue Davis
Nicole Davies
Kelli Proudfoot
Eliza Finn
Karen Ansell
Paisarn Cheewinsiriwat
Anurak Rattachart
Prapaporn Nakwaranon
Kwanthong Pimolaksorn
Prawet Panseetong